Every 20 Years

An Alternative to Congressional Term Limits

By: Thomas E. McDonald

Preface

The partisan natures of our elected officials have put a stranglehold on our government that has never been seen since its founding. Differences have always occurred in the political arena but when it approaches the destruction of the very entity it serves, changes must be made.

The problem that exists in our current government does not lie with the Executive Branch. The problem lies directly and solely with the Legislative Branch. A congress that will not execute the duty that is given them in the first line of the Constitution, "All legislative powers herein granted shall be vested in a congress of the United States . . .," is not fulfilling its constitutional mandate. A congress that will not restrain or challenge the actions of the chief executive based on the rule of law is not a functional body and is not fulfilling the meaning or the function of the separation of powers clause imbedded throughout the Constitution.

A shroud of self serving privilege blankets our elected representatives, both in the House of Representatives and in the Senate. Our Constitutional Founders could not have anticipated their selfish entitlement to privilege. It must end.

What follows offers a solution to the problem of self serving power that permeates the mind-set of the elected members of congress. This is a problem that has swelled and festered for decades. In recent years more and more of the elected representatives have become emboldened and much more blatantly entrenched in their belief they are greater than those who elected them. Congress is, after all a position of civil service. The American people have a right to hold those civil servants to the duties and boundaries of their role.

Term limits are not the answer; and pursuing term limits is a futile gesture. Rather, the proposal presented by Every 20 Years is an alternative to current calls for term limits of the members of the house and senate. Every 20 Years (www.every20years.us) is dedicated to bringing about the end of privilege assumed by the members of our legislative branch of government. In the following pages is a short history and argument as to why change must take place. Herein also is presented a feasible alternative to term limits. This solution needs to be a constitutional amendment establishing a procedure wherein the members of the house and senate would stand for a simple "yes" or "no" retention vote every 20 years. This retention vote is envisioned as a national election. Thereby giving voice to the entire citizenry of this country. Since Congress is entrusted to make the laws that serve the nation as a whole; the whole nation should have its say as to whether or not congress is performing its duties and obligations responsibly. I invite you to read on and support the solution presented by Every 20 years.

Most sincerely,

Thomas E. McDonald
Executive Director,
Every 20 Years

INTRODUCTION

For reasons unknown, our founding fathers did not deem it necessary to impose term limits on members of congress. Perhaps it was their belief that no one would want the job for longer than one or two terms. The founders believed one had a duty to serve when called upon. They also believed that such duty was to be shared by the citizens, willingly or not, and not placed in the hands of a few who would turn such service into a lifelong career or livelihood from which they generated and created great wealth for themselves. Thomas Jefferson spoke of his concern of this in his first inaugural address in 1801:

"Sometimes it is said that man cannot be trusted with the government of himself. Can he, then, be trusted with the government of others?"

Thomas Jefferson: 1st Inaugural Address , 1801.

The current system for electing our representatives to the House and Senate is one that is familiar to all. As for the House of Representatives, Article I, §2, paragraph 1, U.S. Constitution states, *"The House of Representatives shall be composed of Members chosen every second year by the*

People of the several states, and the Electors in each State shall have the qualifications requisite for Electors of the most numerous Branch of the State Legislature".

As regards the Senate, Article 1, §3, paragraph 1, U.S. Constitution states, *"The Senate of the United States shall be composed of two Senators from each State **chosen by the Legislature thereof**, for six Years; and each Senator shall have one vote".* (Emphasis added).

The requirement that Senators be chosen by the state legislators was, of course, changed in 1913 by the Seventeenth Amendment which states: *"The Senate of the United States shall be composed of two Senators from each State, **Elected by the people thereof**, for six years; and each Senator shall have one vote"* (Emphasis added). The amendment was enacted to make Senators more accountable, not only to the citizens of the various states, but also to the United States. The senators were already accountable to the citizens of their respective states, it was the issue of them not being accountable to the country that prompted the change.

It took 124 years to realize the original Constitutional process for choosing Senatorial representation in Congress was flawed and needed changing. Thus the enactment of the Seventeenth Amendment. It has been 100

7

years since a change in the election process of one body of our representatives has occurred. Change is once again needed, if not required, to maintain the representative republic form of government envisioned by those who fought and paid so dearly for our liberty.

Term limiting the members of congress, while not specifically stated in the constitution was a concept that was certainly not foreign to the founding fathers. In 1788 Thomas Jefferson, in a letter to E. Rutledge wrote the following:

"I apprehend too, that the total abandonment of the principle of rotation in the offices of President and Senator will end in abuse. But my confidence is, that there will, for a long time, be virtue and good sense enough in our countrymen, to correct abuses."
Thomas Jefferson to E. Rutledge, July 18, 1788.

As a republic, we have resolved the rotation of the office of President by the 22nd Amendment, which limits the President of the Unites States to two terms. Now is the time to exercise the "virtue and good sense" and implement a process to resolve the rotation of the members of congress. The confidence to correct abuses bequeathed to us by Thomas Jefferson must now be earned.

This government can be a government that is truly representative of the people. The selection process for our congressional representatives, both the house and the senate, must be addressed. After 225 years it has become essential, even necessary, possibly imperative, to implement a change in the election process of our congressional representatives. Over and over again the elected representatives have proven they can no longer be entrusted with the goal of governing for all the citizens rather than a select few. Nor, for that matter, can they be entrusted to passing legislation for all, and selectively exclude themselves. It is time for the citizens of these United States to act -- because congress will not. The key to the regulation of the time served by a member of congress is a vote by the entire populace of the country.

Every 20 Years is founded on the premise that every 20 years all members of the House of Representatives and all members of the Senate stand for a retention vote by the entire country, not just their respective congressional districts and not just their respective states. Consequently, no matter when elected, all 435 members of the House of Representatives and all 100 members of the Senate could be voted out of office every 20 years.

I - The New Aristocracy

The Issue

In 2009, a small group of Republican senators proposed a constitutional amendment to limit how long an elected member of congress would serve in office. This group of Senators was led by the now retired Sen. Jim DeMint of South Carolina. The group called for a cap of 12 years in office for senators and six years in office for members of the House. Not surprisingly the measure did not get the required two-thirds approval from the House and Senate to pass and be sent to the states to begin the ratification process. This is but the latest attempt to impose term limits on the members of congress.

A similar term limit measure known as the *Citizen Legislature Act* was a part of the original *Contract with America* proposed by Newt Gingrich led Republicans in 1994. Paragraph ten of the Contract stated,

10. THE CITIZEN LEGISLATURE ACT: A first-ever vote on term limits to replace career politicians with citizen legislators.

Contract with America, 1994

Again, not surprisingly, this measure also failed to get the needed support. It is safe to assert that members of congress will never vote to limit their terms as every attempt to limit the terms of the members of congress has failed. Now is the time the citizens must act and retake the republic.

In a Gallup Poll released January 11, 2013 regarding term limits for members of congress, 75% of those polled indicated they would vote in favor of term limits if given the opportunity. However, as is usually most evident, individuals are always more willing to limit the terms of someone else's congressperson, but not their own.

Sadly, the members of congress have become the aristocracy of the United States. They are the same class of English nobility against whom the colonists waged war from 1775-1782 to secure a free country based on a rule of law and not of men. John Adams recognized this issue in 1772:

"When the whole Power of the Society is lodged in the Hands of the whole Society, the Government is called a Democracy, or the Rule of the Many. When the Sovereignty, or Supreme Power is placed in the Hands of a few great, rich, wise Men, the Government is an Aristocracy, or the Rule of the few."

John Adams, (spring 1772),

Notes for an oration at Braintree.

Because of the aristocratic status they have assumed, and one they so desperately try to maintain, it is not surprising that any suggestion or proposal to limit their term fails to develop support among our elected representatives in congress. And it is somewhat understandable. Ask yourself, why would they end their own reign? If given the opportunity, who among us would fire ourselves, or vote ourselves out of a position equal to that of royalty and accompanied with the benefits and privileges of royalty?

The fact that Congress has evolved to this class of pseudo aristocracy is not shocking. Human nature rarely shocks or surprises. This was a concern of our founding fathers and was contemplated and foreseen by many of them. Thomas Jefferson foresaw such an eventuality over 225 years ago when he wrote to William Smith from Paris on November 13, 1787 in what has become known as his Tree of Liberty Letter. He wrote in part:

"God forbid we should ever be twenty years without such a rebellion. The people cannot be all, and always, well informed. The part which is wrong will be discontented, in proportion to the importance of the facts they misconceive. If they remain quiet under such misconceptions, it is lethargy, the forerunner of death to the public liberty.... And what country can preserve its liberties, if its

rulers are not warned from time to time, that this people preserve the spirit of resistance? Let them take arms. The remedy is to set them right as to the facts, pardon and pacify them. What signify a few lives lost in a century or two? The tree of liberty must be refreshed from time to time, with the blood of patriots and tyrants. It is its natural manure."

Thomas Jefferson, Letter to
William S. Smith,
November 13, 1787

We are well beyond the *"twenty years"* advocated by Jefferson. Ten times twenty years beyond. And perhaps the reason is his phrase about *"the blood of patriots"* being shed. A great quantity of blood was shed to obtain our independence and a great quantity of blood has been shed to preserve our independence. But it may not be necessary to actually shed blood. The language of Jefferson can be tempered by implementing a means and method whereby there would be no need for shedding *"the blood of patriots."* Citizens need to ensure that *"this country can preserve its liberties."* But, as the first three words of the Preamble to the Constitution so powerfully states, it up to us, *"We the People . . ."*

We the people are disappointed and frustrated with our congress. Even angry with our congress. Plain and simple, we the people do not believe congress is doing the job they are elected to do, representing the people of this country in a manner proscribed by the Preamble to the United States Constitution, establish justice, insure domestic tranquility, provide for the common defense, promote the general welfare, and secures the blessings of Liberty to ourselves and our posterity, . . .

Consider that the job approval rating of congress is at an all time low. Data from recent polls dating to October 17, 2013, as reported by *Real Clear Politics,* shows that on average approximately 75% of those individuals polled disapprove of the job congress is doing.

Real Clear Politics
Congressional Job Approval
Polling Data

Poll	Date	Approve	Disapprove	Spread
RCP Average	10/17 - 12/2	9.1	84.6	-75.5
The Economist/YouGov	11/30 - 12/2	6	73	-67
CBS News	11/15 - 11/18	11	85	-74
FOX News	11/10 - 11/12	10	85	-75
Gallup	11/7 - 11/10	9	86	-77
National Journal	11/2 - 11/6	9	84	-75
GWU/Battleground	10/27 - 10/31	9	87	-78
CNN/Opinion Research	10/18 - 10/20	10	88	-78
ABC News/Wash Post	10/17 - 10/20	9	89	-80

These poll numbers do not, however, appear to have any influence on the members of congress as they continue to act first and foremost in their own best interest. Congress does not fear the voting public. In the workplaces of America, an evaluation wherein an individual is deemed to be doing their job favorably only 25% of the time would, and should, result in termination. Or, at the very least, such poor performance rating should lead to the implementation of a process wherein termination would result if the poor performance continued uncorrected.

But again, the complaints that resonate throughout the constituency of the various congressional districts and states that members of congress are not doing their job are usually directed at the representatives and senators from other districts and states. Year in and year out, we have heard these assertions; we may have uttered these assertions. Yet there is no evidence of action by the people. The majority of people rarely condemn the representatives or senators from their own district or state.

Under the current system, complaining is ineffective and futile unless it is inclusive of each complainant's own representative and senator, as well as those of others. Think about it, congress receives abysmal approval ratings yet the members continually get re-elected. Most times their re-election is to the detriment of the United States as a whole.

The additional complaint that our congressional representatives are wealthy millionaires is not the fault of the Constitution. Rather, the blame lies with us, the voters. As a people, we elect the rich and wealthy to congress, and continually re-elect them. This is the very destructive pattern that opens the door to a privileged class of representatives, an aristocracy if you will. Our elected representatives enact laws that represent the needs and desires of the rich and wealthy, rather than the citizens. Our elected representatives believe they are not accountable to the citizens of the Unites States, only to the special interests groups that elect them from their respective district or state.

George Washington purposely set a precedent of serving only two terms as president. It was not written, nor was it decreed that as president, George Washington was to serve only two terms. It was custom and practice, initiated by Washington that became tradition. As a tradition, it lasted for one hundred and forty four years. It was Franklin D. Roosevelt who cast this custom, practice and tradition aside in 1941 and again in 1945 when he was sworn in for his third and fourth terms respectively. This happened because there was no written directive or limitation recorded to inhibit him from dismissing that long standing tradition. Franklin D. Roosevelt ignored established custom and practice for personal gain.

What Franklin D. Roosevelt did in the office of the presidency the members of congress do every election cycle. Because limits were not written down, we have representatives and senators who have served, and are continuing to serve, well beyond what was contemplated or envisioned by our founding fathers. Our congressional representatives have remained in office to the point where their myopic vision serves only themselves, and those similarly situated, not the people of their respective states and especially not the people of these United States. Those many career malingerers are no longer our representatives, they are our modern day, self anointed aristocracy.

With the exception of Carl Hayden of Arizona, who began serving in the House of Representatives in 1912, and continued in the senate from 1927 to 1969, a total of 57 years in both houses, and Richard Russell of Georgia, who served from 1933 – 1971, (38 years in the senate) the remaining eight of the top ten longest serving Senators all began their tenures subsequent to the term of Franklin D. Roosevelt. Sadly, the attitude of self deserving and self serving appears to have originated with President Roosevelt. This misaligned mindset stems from the point that if the president can cast aside custom and tradition and serve for as long as he or she desired, why not our representatives and senators?

Due to a fear of the potential abuse that was foreseen by the four terms of President Franklin Roosevelt, and the possibility any president could establish a quasi-dictatorship, the 22nd Amendment to the Constitution was proposed and ratified in 1951 setting forth that *"no person shall be elected to the office of the President more than twice, and no person who has held the office of President , or acted as President, for more than two years of a term to which some other person was elected President shall be elected to the office of the President more than once."*

It is now time to establish a similar law that applies to the members of congress.

Consider the following list of the longest serving current members of the U.S. Senate:

1. Patrick Leahy, (D) Vermont - began serving January 3, 1975 - (38 years)

2. Orrin Hatch, (R) Utah – began serving January 3, 1977 - (36 years)

3. Max Baucus, (D) Montana – began serving December 15, 1978 – (35 years)

4. Thad Cochran, (R) Mississippi – began serving December 27, 1978 – (35 years)

5. Carl Levin, (D) Michigan – began serving January 3, 1979 – (34 years)

6. Charles Grassley, (R) Iowa – began serving January 3, 1981 – (32 years)

7. Tom Harkin, (D) Iowa – began serving January 3, 1985 – (28 years)

8. Mitch McConnell, (R) Kentucky – began serving January 3, 1985 – (28 years)

9. Jay Rockefeller, (D) West Virginia – began serving January 15, 1985 – (28 years)

10. Barbara Mikulski, (D) Maryland – began serving January 3, 1987 – (26 years)

Remarkably, these ten current members of the U.S. Senate to date have served a total of 320 years. Because they are still serving in office, this startling number will continue to rise mercurially as certain of them seek re-election.

Following is the all time top ten list of the longest serving members of the U.S. Senate:

1. Robert Byrd, (D) West Virginia, 1959-2010- 51 year 5 months, 26 days

2. Daniel Inouye, (D) Hawaii, 1963-2001 – 49 years, 11 months, 15 days*

3. Strom Thurmond (R) S. Carolina, 1954-2003 – 47 years, 5 months, 8days

4. Ted Kennedy (D) Massachusetts, 1962-2009 – 46 years, 9 months, 19 days

5. Carl Hayden (D) Arizona, 1927-1969 – 41 years, 9 months, 30 days **

6. John Stennis (D) Mississippi, 1947-1989 – 41 years, 1 month, 29 days

7. Ted Stevens (R) Alaska, 1968-2009 – 40 years, 10
    days
8. Patrick Leahy (D) Vermont, 1975 – present
9. Ernest Hollings (D) S. Carolina, 1966-2005 – 38 years,
    1 month, 25 days
10. Richard Russell (D) Georgia, 1933-1971 – 38 years,
    19 days.

> * Daniel Inouye also served in the House of
> Representatives   from 1959 – 1963
> ** Carl Hayden also served in the House of
> Representatives   from 1912-1927

The ten longest serving members of the senate have served a total of 428 + years and because Senator Leahy of Vermont is currently in office, this number will also increase.

Below is the list of the ten longest serving current members of the U.S. House of Representatives:

1. John Dingell, (D) Michigan – began serving December
    13, 1955 – (58 years)
2. John Conyers, Jr., (D) Michigan – began serving January 3,
    1965 – (48 years)
3. Charles B. Rangel, (D) New York – began serving January 3,
    1971 – (42 years)
4. Don Young, (R) Alaska – began serving March 6, 1971 – (42
    years)

5.   George Miller, (D) California – began serving January 3, 1975
     – (38 years)

6.   Henry Waxman, (D) California – began serving January 3,
     1975 – (38 years)

7.   Nick Rahall II, (D) West Virginia – began serving January 3,
     1977 – (36 years)

8.   Jim Sensenbrenner, (R) Wisconsin – began serving January 3,
     1979 – (34 years)

9.   Tom Petri, (R) Wisconsin – began serving April 3, 1979 – (34
     years)

10. Ralph M. Hall, (R) Texas – began serving January 3, 1981 –
     (32 years)

These ten current members of the U.S. House of Representatives have served a total of 402 years in aggregate, and because they are still serving in office, this number will continue to rise as certain of them seek re-election.

The list that follows is of the top ten longest serving members of the House of Representatives:

1.   John Dingell, (D) Michigan – 58 years (December 13, 1955 -
     current)

2.   Jamie L. Whitten, (D) Mississippi – 53 years (Nov. 4, 1941 to
     Jan. 3, 1995)

3.   Carl Vinson, (D) Georgia – 50 years (November 3, 1914, to
     January 3, 1965

4.   Emanuel Cellars (D) New York –49 years (March 1923 to
     January 1973)

5. John Conyers, (D) Michigan – 49 years (January 3, 1965 - current)

6. Sam Rayburn, (D) Tennessee – 48 years – (March 4, 1913 – November 16, 1961)

7. Sidney Yates, (D) Illinois – 48 years (1949 to 1963 and 1965 to 1999)

8. Wright Patman, (D) Texas– 47 years (March 4, 1929 – March 7, 1976)

9. Adolph Sabath, (D) Illinois – 45 years (March 4, 1907 - November 1952)

10. George H. Mahon, (D) Texas – 44 years (January 3, 1935 – January 3, 1979)

The ten longest serving members of congress have served a total of 491 years and because two of the names on the list, John Dingell and John Conyers, are currently in office, this number will also increase.

It is highly questionable whether the longevity of these members, both current and past, has benefited the state or district represented by the said member of congress; if it has benefited the United States as a whole; or if it has primarily benefited the individual office holder.

In examining these lists, there is no degree of certainty that the very lengthy terms of these representatives and senators has resulted in any improvement in the quality of life of its citizens, or the improvement of the quality of government. Ask yourself these questions:

Did their tenure result in better government?

Did their tenure result in poorer government?

Does such a protracted tenure result in legislation that would not have been achieved or accomplished by anyone other than these elected individuals?

Did they bring to their respective house of congress ideas and talents that no one else possessed?

Obviously these questions are nearly impossible to answer. But then so too is the question:

Could some other individual have performed the duties of that office that might have provided more benefits for this government, this country and its citizens?

It is time to implement a procedure that would lead to possible answers to these impossible questions. And this procedure must include the threat of potential term limitation.

II - Term Regulation, Not Term Limitation

The Premise

The founding fathers drafted a document that was applicable to the United States as a whole, not the individual states. The new country had tried, and found wanting, Articles of Confederation. The **Articles of Confederation** were a written agreement ratified by the original thirteen states in 1781 to provide a legal symbol of their union by withholding from the central government coercive power over the states or their citizens. The basic premise of the Articles of Confederation was that each state would maintain its own sovereignty and all rights to govern, except those rights specifically granted by Congress. The purpose of the Articles was to establish a weak central government but yet also prevent the states from individually conducting their own foreign diplomacy. The states were quite adamant in wanting to keep the federal government as weak as possible, limiting it to only those explicit powers involving national defense and general welfare of the citizens. The founding fathers feared a government that would usurp the individual power of the states. Each state cherished its independence and wanted to maintain it. The confederation concept obviously did not work. Consequently, the Constitution was drafted to replace the Articles of Confederation and the new Constitution became effective March 4, 1789. The change was an attempt to create a "more perfect union", as so stated in the preamble to the Constitution:

"We the People of the United States, in Order (sic) to form a more perfect union, establish justice, insure domestic Tranquility, provide for the common defense, promote the general welfare, and secure the Blessings of Liberty to ourselves and our Posterity, do ordain and establish this Constitution of the United States of America".

This preamble to the Constitution has been read countless times by high school students in civic classes, college students in political science classes and laws students in Constitutional Law courses, as well as numerous legal scholars but, because it is not considered a part of the Constitution itself is usually considered merely an introduction to what follows in the Constitution. It is much more than that. It is the commanding introduction to a constitution that establishes a very unique form of government.

The following paraphrases the Articles, sections, and paragraphs of the U.S. Constitution that set forth the foundation of representation of the states in the federal system.

Article I, § 1 vests the legislative power in a Congress of the Unites States consisting of a Senate and House of Representatives.

Article I, § 2, ¶ 1 states that the House of Representatives shall be composed of Members chosen every two years by the people of the several states. There is no constraint or prohibition   for "un-choosing" Members of the House.

Article I, § 2, ¶ 2 sets out age requirements and citizenship requirements of the United States, and merely requires a member of the House of Representatives be an "inhabitant of the state in which he (sic) shall be chosen". Note, it states "inhabitant", not citizen. This is important.

Article I, § 2, ¶ 4 requires that when a vacancy occurs in the House from any state, the Executive Authority of that state shall issue Writs of Election to fill the vacancy. In other words, the governor of the state cannot, and shall not, appoint a replacement but rather the people shall vote on that replacement no matter how short the remaining term.

Article I, §3, ¶ 1 states the Senate of the Unites States shall be composed of two Senators from each state chosen by the Legislature thereof, for six years; and each senator shall have one vote.

In 1913, this method of selection for senators was changed by the Seventeenth Amendment, which required that subsequent to the effective date of the Seventeenth Amendment, each Senator would thereafter be elected by the people of each state.

Article I, § 3, ¶ 3 sets out the age requirements of each senator and the requirement of citizenry of the United States, and reiterates, like members of the House or Representatives, a member of the Senate need not be a citizen of the state from whence chosen, but merely an "inhabitant".

The Constitution does not require a condition that any person that is elected to the office of representative, or chosen senator, be a citizen of the state from which elected or chosen. This "condition", and it is clear that it is a condition, can be read that it was the intent of the framers of the constitution that neither a member of the House or Senate was required to be a citizen of the district or state they represented because they were not representing only their district or state. They were also representing the United States. Their representation was not exclusive to a specific district or state; it was much broader. Also significant, there is no mention of term limits in Article I.

Every 20 Years believes it would not be a panacea to solely impose term limits on our elected congressional representatives. There must be something more, there must be an alternative to term limits.

As of January 2013 there are 15 states that have passed laws limiting the terms of their elected legislative representatives. In the chart depicted below from the *National Conference of State Legislatures* the last column calls out the percentage of citizens who voted for legislative term limits. It is noteworthy in that:

- six of those fifteen states tallied 70% or more of yes votes,
- five of the fifteen states tallied 60 % or more of yes votes and
- only four of the fifteen states were in the 50% range.

It is noteworthy again that two of those four states in the 50% range were at 59.9% and 58.8% respectively. These high percentages are significant in that they clearly demonstrate strong feelings among the electorate of those states that term limitation of elected officials is an important issue.

State	Year Enacted	House		Senate		% Voted Yes
		Limit	Year of Impact	Limit	Year of Impact	
MAINE	1993	8	1996	8	1996	67.6
CALIFORNIA	1990	12 (c)	1996	12 (c)	1998	52.2
COLORADO	1990	8	1998	8	1998	71
ARKANSAS	1992	6	1998	8	2000	59.9
MICHIGAN	1992	6	1998	8	2002	58.8
FLORIDA	1992	8	2000	8	2000	76.8
OHIO	1992	8	2000	8	2000	68.4
SOUTH DAKOTA	1992	8	2000	8	2000	63.5
MONTANA	1992	8	2000	8	2000	67
ARIZONA	1992	8	2000	8	2000	74.2
MISSOURI	1992	8	2002	8	2002	75

(a)						
OKLAHOMA	1990	12 (c)	2004	12 (c)	2004	67.3
NEBRASKA	2000	n/a	n/a	8	2006	56
LOUISIANA	1995	12	2007	12	2007	76
NEVADA (b)	1996	12	2010	12	2010	70.4

Source: National Conference of State Legislatures

The chart is very indicative that the citizens of the various states wanted term limits. However, when those term limits are reached, the outgoing office holder merely moves on to another office. For example, members of a State House of Representatives will declare for the State Senate, or vice versa. Others will pursue a seat on a county governing body as a member of a county board of supervisors, while others will chase positions on a city council or perhaps a mayoral position. Still others will chase other state wide office such as Secretary of State or Treasurer, or even Governor. Action to pursue other such elected offices may be interpreted as an unquenchable desire to serve the constituency, but a more accurate assessment is one that it is the desire to continue feeding at the public trough to maintain status and hold onto the perks and semi-aristocratic lifestyles. It is most conceivable that what term limits have wrought at the state level would be no different at the national level. And a very real possibility is that a term limited member of congress would gladly accept a position of lobbyist to maintain that lifestyle.

Any discussion of term limitation of elected officials must be premised with questions of fairness. Is it fair to implement term limits? And if it is, how is the implementation of terms to be regulated? Is a limit of two terms fair for each representative and each senator? Since the term of a United States Representative is two years and the term of a United States Senator is 6 years it hardly seems equitable that a member of the House of Representatives should be limited to a total of 4 years (two terms) while a member of the Senate would be "entitled" to 12 years. In fairness, perhaps the limitation should be expressed in years rather than terms. Rather than two terms, it would be 12 years. But then this would give rise to concern of a member of the House of Representatives having to endure 6 elections cycles while a senator only two. Again, not fair. As the various scenarios are discerned, the terms proposed all include questions of fairness and it will probably always be an issue.

It is imperative there be a balance between what a member of congress does for their constituency and what he/she does for their country. Congressmen and

Congresswomen are elected to do both, but the latter has been sorely neglected, and arguably, almost completely abandoned. This must be corrected, and it is why the current system needs to be changed. Merely establishing term limits will not change the system or the practice.

III - Every 20 Years

The Solution

There are two important distinctions between the term limit of the President and any proposed term limits for members of congress. Both can be term limited to one term by failing to get re-elected. The President under any circumstance is definitely limited to two terms. The second distinction is the election of the president is by the entire country. It is the second distinction that is the key to limiting the terms of the members of congress, a vote by the entire populace of the country. At some point, our congressional representatives must submit to election by the entire country and not only their respective districts of states.

Every 20 Years is the organization founded to advance this solution that every 20 years the entire House of Representative and the entire Senate should stand for a retention vote by the entire country. The vote cannot be based on just a voter's respective congressional districts or just their respective states. By implementing the Every 20 Year solution, no matter when elected, all 435 members of the House of Representatives and all 100 members of the Senate, could be voted out of office, every 20 years. It is not an absolute certainty they would be voted out of office, it is merely a possibility.

It is important to emphasize that this 20 years is not a limitation on congressional terms per se; it is only a limitation if the members of congress choose it to be a term limitation. It is through their personal conduct and the quality of their service to the country that would cause a limitation of their terms. Essentially their job performance, as perceived by the populace of the country, would be the critical factor in determining whether or not each elected member of congress would be retained or not.

Our elected representatives are the employees of the people of these United States. As was posed earlier, what employee would fire themselves from their employment? Consequently, it is incumbent upon the employer, we the people, to terminate those employees when the job they do is opposed to the good of the country and its inhabitants. The majority of individuals in this country work very hard to keep their employment. The ways in which retained employment is accomplished is by performing the duties and responsibilities of the position conscientiously and working on behalf of, and to the satisfaction of their supervisor, employers, bosses, company, or stockholders. Whatever label fits. An employee is subject to periodic evaluation. And it is time an evaluation be done on our congressional representatives. The ultimate consequence for a negative evaluation for congress would, and should, result in termination of all elected official per the Every 20 Year solution.

Every 20 years the entire House of Representative and the entire Senate should stand for a retention vote by the entire country—not just by their respective congressional districts and not just their respective states. No matter when elected, all 435 members of the House of Representatives and all 100 members of the Senate could feasibly be voted out of office every 20 years.

At first blush, this may sound harsh, but a reading Article I, § 8, paragraphs1-18 makes it quite evident that congress does not do the job as visualized by those who fought and died to establish our government. Their sacrifice should not be diminished by self serving, self absorbed representatives.

The enumerated powers set forth in Article 1, § 8, paragraphs1-18 of the Constitution give congress the power to pass certain laws that apply to all the citizens of the United States, not just the citizens of the respective districts or state of each individual member of the House of Representatives or each individual member of the Senate. As such, as to these powers, each member of congress should be, and must be, held accountable to all of the citizens of the

United States. These enumerated powers are explicitly set forth as follows:

Article 1, § 8

1. The Congress shall have Power To lay and collect Taxes, Duties, Imposts and Excises, to pay the Debts and provide for the common Defense and general Welfare of the United States; but all Duties, Impostsand Excises shall be uniform throughout the United States;

2. To borrow Money on the credit of the United States;

3. To regulate Commerce with foreign Nations, and among the several States, and with the Indian Tribes;

4. To establish a uniform Rule of Naturalization, and uniform Laws on the subject of Bankruptcies throughout the United States;

5. To coin Money, regulate the Value thereof, and of foreign Coin, and fix the Standard of Weights and Measures;

6. To provide for the Punishment of counterfeiting the Securities and current Coin of the United States;

7. To establish Post Offices and post Roads;

8. To promote the Progress of Science and useful Arts, by securing for limited Times to

Authors and Inventors the exclusive Right to their respective Writings and Discoveries;

9. To constitute Tribunals inferior to the Supreme Court;

10. To define and punish Piracies and Felonies committed on the high Seas, and Offences against the Law of Nations;

11. To declare War, grant Letters of Marque and Reprisal, and make Rules concerning Captures on Land and Water;

12. To raise and support Armies, but no Appropriation of Money to that Use shall be for a longer Term than two Years;

13. To provide and maintain a Navy;

14. To make Rules for the Government and Regulation of the land and naval Forces;

15. To provide for calling forth the Militia to execute the Laws of the Union, suppress Insurrections and repel Invasions;

16. To provide for organizing, arming, and disciplining, the Militia, and for governing such Part of them as may be employed in the Service of the United States, reserving to the States respectively, the Appointment of the Officers, and the Authority of training the Militia according to the discipline prescribed by Congress;

17. To exercise exclusive Legislation in all Cases whatsoever, over such District (not exceeding ten Miles square) as may, by Cession of

particular States, and the Acceptance of Congress, become the Seat of the Government of the United States, and to exercise like Authority over all Places purchased by the Consent of the Legislature of the State in which the Same shall be, for the Erection of Forts, Magazines, Arsenals, dock-Yards, and other needful Buildings;-- And

18.   To make all Laws which shall be necessary and proper for carrying into Execution the foregoing Powers, and all other Powers vested by this Constitution in the Government of the United States, or in any Department or Officer thereof.

Even a cursory reading of the enumerated powers should reveal that these powers constitute the scope and limit of congressional authority, as granted by we the people. These enumerated powers verify there is not one such power that relates specifically and solely to any one individual state or any one specific district. Understand then that Congressional representatives are mandated by the United States Constitution to represent the country as whole before and above their individual district or state. We the people must insist our government uphold this very basic premise and by doing so it becomes a gage of performance by the body of those elected officials in congress.

With the scope of powers in mind, examine again the

Articles of Confederation which reveal the federal government was created to serve a very limited purpose, with the majority of power left to individual states. Remember, when these Articles were found inadequate to serve its intended purpose, the constitution was proposed and ratified to take its place. The constitution was conceived to improve upon the Articles of Confederation, and one brilliant facet remained abundantly clear, the majority of sovereign power was to remain with the states, not transferred to the federal government. When the constitution did not live up to this goal, the Bill of Rights (the first ten amendments) were proposed and ratified in 1791. Most noteworthy, the tenth amendment again made it even clearer that any power not delegated to the United States was reserved to the states.

"The powers not delegated to the United States by the Constitution, nor prohibited by it to the States, are reserved to the States respectively, or to the people."

Tenth Amendment to the U.S. Constitution (1791)

Why this emphasis on the division of power between the federal government and the states? Essentially there are two basic structural components of the American constitutional system. One is the Separation of powers between the three branches of government, and the other is federalism, the governmental powers divided between a central government, Washington D.C., and a set of regional or territorial governments, the states.

The original concept of federalism envisioned by the framers of the constitution was one of dual federalism, a governmental process in which the national government and the state government exercised authority within separate, self contained areas of public policy, public administration, and public good. However, this theory of dual federalism has evolved over the decades to a modern approach of cooperative federalism in which power is shared among national, state and local authorities. Areas that were once exclusive to the state and local governments are now being infringed upon by the federal government.

Our government has moved beyond dual federalism and cooperative federalism and the current trends have our country in the throes of coercive federalism, wherein the federal government uses its powers to induce and coerce states to adopt policies they would otherwise not adopt. We have transformed from the ideal concept of dual federalism to cooperative federalism and now to coercive federalism. This coercive federalism is implemented by congress in various ways, including the supremacy clause, the commerce clause and the necessary and proper clause, along with its spending powers. This unhealthy transformation, this conversion, cannot stand if this country is to remain a representative republic as was intended. This transformation will certainly continue if congress continues to operate in its current manner. If this course remains unaltered, this country will crumble. Change is necessary now. It is the citizens, acting through the power of the individual states who must provide the impetus to ensure congressional representatives serve their country first, their state or district second, and most importantly, their self interest not at all.

If the entire body of Congress, all 535 members, were to stand for retention on a periodic basis by the entire citizenry of the United States, the entire country would have a voice in the type of government it wants, needs, and deserves. How can this county have a future with anything less. As each twenty year retention cycle approaches, it is envisioned each member of congress would abandon their personal pursuits of power and riches, the short sighted interests of their respective districts or states, and look to their duty, their obligation and their responsibility of representing the United States of America. In short, it should spur them on to do the job they were elected to do. Failure to do so would result in forcing them to abdicate their congressional thrones. This country is the Unites States of America, not the Divided States of America.

IV -- Term Regulation, Not Term Limits

The Strategy

The last time the issue of term limits came before congress in 2009 in the form of a constitutional amendment, the stumbling block, or the perceived stumbling block, was that two-thirds of the House and Senate would not approve such an amendment. That is what would be required for such an amendment to become part of the constitution. At least that is what the members of congress would have you believe.

This issue of term limits, or term regulation, is so critical to the future of this country that it cannot be left up to congress. The initiative of the people must make this happen. And, in their wisdom, the founding fathers foresaw that at some point a potential conflict would arise wherein the members of congress and the people of the United States would be at odds. They knew the constitution would have to be amended to resolve the conflict. Because of the potential conflict the founding fathers provided two methods for amending the constitution, not just one. They did not want to leave the sole means of curtailing the abuses of a radical and self-serving congress to that congress itself.

The framers of the Constitution made provision for the constitution to be amended, but they did not make it easy. Article V of the Constitution states:

*The Congress, whenever two thirds of both Houses shall deem it necessary, shall propose **Amendments to this Constitution, or, on the Application of the Legislatures of two thirds of the several States,** shall call a Convention for proposing Amendments, which, in either Case, shall be valid to all Intents and Purposes, as Part of this Constitution, when ratified by the Legislatures of three fourths of the several States, or by Conventions in three fourths thereof, as the one or the other Mode of Ratification may be proposed by the Congress; Provided that no Amendment which may be made prior to the Year One thousand eight hundred and eight shall in any Manner affect the first and fourth Clauses in the Ninth Section of the first Article; and that no State, without its Consent, shall be deprived of its equal Suffrage in the Senate.* **(Emphasis added)**

If congress will not call for a constitutional amendment they shall, and the key word is shall, meaning they have no choice or alternatives, call a convention upon the application of the legislatures of two thirds of the states. To date, in the entire history of this country, only the first method has been used. If ever a time existed wherein the second method could and should be used, it is now. We need not wait for, or rely on congress to bring this matter of term limits, or term regulation, to the people. To rely on the members of congress to address the issue of term limits or term regulation would be futile as they have opposed all prior attempts.

Term regulation is an issue that must be presented to the States, by the citizens, requesting the legislature of each state to call for a constitutional convention. As congress will not act, the states must. This is how the Every 20 Year's solution must be implemented.

To fully understand the meaning and intent behind Article V a reading of the Federalist papers is required. In Federalist paper # 39, attributed to James Madison, the fourth President of the United States, Madison sets out the concept of the country being both federal and national in nature. Federal in the sense of the congress, National in the sense of the people. It could not be totally Federal; it could not be totally National. If it were totally Federal all states would have to agree to change, if it were totally National, then only a simple majority of the people would be required to alter the government. As it is, two-thirds of the states are required for the calling of a constitutional convention. Three-fourths of the states or three-fourths of congress is required for ratification of an amendment.

The power lies with the states. This was intentional. Recall again that the Articles of Confederation vested power in the states. Under the constitution, power was entrusted to the federal government, power the federal government did not have previously under the Articles of Confederation. However, the caveat in turning power over to the federal government was to retain sufficient power by the states to amend the constitution should it ever become necessary to do so. And now it is necessary to do so.

This power of the states to call for a constitutional convention must now be utilized to transform and limit the terms of the elected representatives in congress. Perhaps term limits is an option, but it does not offer the purging that the Every 20 Years solution offers. In the event term limits is deemed inapplicable, limitation by constitutional amendment must present conditions, conditions that would adhere to the Federal/National concept espoused by James Madison in Federalist # 39.

Adhering to the time frame proposed by Thomas Jefferson in his "Tree of Liberty" letter to William Smith in 1787, it is suggested that the twenty year "revolution" take place at the ballot box rather than by armed conflict, and in such a manner that would result in the entire body of congress, the 435 members of the House of Representatives and the 100 members of the Senate would stand for a simple yes or no retention vote. The exclusive issue presented in the Every 20 Years vote is whether or not congress, as a body, should be retained.

A constitutional amendment can accomplish the Every 20 Years solution. This is the process, the process that would implement a yes or no retention vote of each and every one of our elected representatives and senators. As with any process, it is the details that define the process. As for those details, suggestions follow in Part V.

The need for the Every 20 Years solution arrived sometime ago. The 535 individuals who occupy the desks and offices in our capital as our alleged representatives must be put on notice that they do in fact represent this country, they do in fact represent its citizens and that their failure to do so will result in their replacement. Others are fully capable of taking up these elected offices and representing this country. Not one of the current elected officials in office is irreplaceable.

V - The Retention Vote

Implementing the Process

The replacement of 535 elected representatives is not as daunting as it sounds. The process is almost entirely in place already. Final implementation needs only a few additional steps.

Twenty years subsequent to the ratification of the amendment, and coinciding with a normal election year of members of congress, such retention vote would be held on the 1st Tuesday following the first Monday of October. The date of the first retention vote would be set by the Amendment, held on that date, and then held every 20 years thereafter.

The question on the ballot put before the voters would be simple and one in number: Should the 535 members of congress be retained? If the majority vote would be in the affirmative, then the members of congress would retain their respective seats and stand for election and re-election under the current system of election laws. There would be no retention vote held for another 20 years when the process would once more be put into operation.

The advantage of the retention vote is that this is not

a limitation on the term of any elected representative as they hold the key as to whether or not they would be retained. If they continue to vote purely personal and self serving interests, if they continue to exempt themselves from all laws passed, or even one of the laws passed, this disregard for the purpose of the office they hold would be a clear and convincing indication that they fear nothing--even the retention vote of the people. It is for this reason such a retention vote is required.

The retention vote would be by simple majority. No electoral college vote, just a simple yes or no vote on whether the sitting members of congress as of the date of the vote should be retained in office.

If the majority vote was no, that the members of congress should not be retained, all members of congress would be out of office effective immediately. Effective immediately would mean within 24 hours of the vote. Immediately subsequent to a vote of no, the sitting representatives would have no power to propose or vote on any legislation. They would be divested of all constitutional powers and privileges held while in office.

Following this vote of no, the normal election process would be held, meaning that the November election would go forth as scheduled, but it would be for the election of all 535 members of congress, 435 to the House of Representatives and 100 to the Senate. Those representatives and senators that had been voted out would not be allowed to run for election to their former office until after one full election cycle for their seat had elapsed.

Any citizen meeting the criteria as set out in Article I of the Constitution as to the qualifications of members of the House of Representatives and Senators, as amended by the Seventeenth Amendment, would be eligible to run as a candidate in the November election for the vacated seats. Each candidate would have one week to declare their candidacy, and the remaining time to campaign. There would no limitation on the number of individuals who could run. The individual with the most votes on the November election date would be declared the winner of the election and entitled to the seat to which elected. There would no runoff election except in the event of a tie between any candidates.

The newly elected representatives would proceed through the process as is currently in place and sworn into their respective office on January 1 of the following year.

At first blush it may appear this process would proceed at breakneck speed, and that would be true. However, there are several significant benefits to this expedited process, the least of which is the curtailing of the influence of big money and, more importantly, dark money, and the influence of special interest groups.

The large moneyed special interest groups that currently pour millions of dollars into the campaign coffers of candidates would be severely restricted by the short time frames and constraints as the replacement process proceeds forward. Because of the uncertainty of an affirmative retention vote the moneyed special interests groups would be reluctant to bestow huge sums of money on sitting members of congress who may not be retained in office. Moreover, because of the uncertainty of the sitting congress being turned out, they also would be hindered in raising money from the large moneyed special interests groups and lobbying firms.

Likewise, should the entire congress be turned out, the moneyed special interests would have little time to "buy" a candidates loyalty.

These benefits take a large portion of "big money" out of politics and put the selection process in the hands of the citizens, where it should be.

To preserve the integrity of this October retention vote, all eligible voters would be required to have an identification voter card. If this is set by amendment, the sitting members of congress who refuse to address this issue for fear of alienating certain groups or special interests, would be saved the discomfort of actually making it known how they feel about voter registration identification cards. It would be a settled matter. The amendment would require the voter identification card to vote in the retention election, and all subsequent elections. No card, no vote, period.

An additional benefit to the expedited election process would be that those in office, facing a possible eviction from their office, would hopefully see the advantage of governing for the country as a whole rather than just their constituents or more precisely, just for themselves. It should be an end to their attempts to keep their position as an aristocrat. Of course, the very nature of the Every 20 Years solution would make it apparent they would have to begin this process several years before the election and not several months or weeks to be effective. The results would be a better informed and responsive congress, and a better and more viable country.

This very quick election cycle would have several advantages to the country. Examine a summary of the advantages:

1. The election procedures and infrastructure is already in place in the respective states and precincts.
2. An expedited election period.

3. Curtailing the influence of PACs, well financed lobbyists, unions, and dark money interests.

4. Force the candidates to spell out quickly and precisely how they would change the government from that of their predecessors.

5. Force the candidates to spell out how they intend not only to represent their constituents but also the citizens of the entire country. Both are possible and it would be their job to quickly articulate to the American people how they intend to accomplish it.

6. Eliminate any lame duck session by having the congress not so retained, evacuating their office within two weeks, thereby eliminating any opportunity to meet as a coercive governing body during the evacuation process.

7. Eliminate the "bridges to nowhere" and strive to have "bridges to somewhere"

8. Have a government for the people and by the people; and not for political parties and by special interests.

9. Increase national voter participation to effectuate real change, and not just change in name only but actual change in governmental processes.

10. Less corruption. With the expedited election window of only 30 days the special interests would be reluctant to spend money not needed as the retention vote could be one for retention and not for eviction.

This process obviously raises the question of who governs during this period of time that a sitting congress would be rejected and the new replacement congress takes their oath of office. This time period would be approximately 90 days.

An examination of the actual number of days spent by the congress between election day and the swearing day of the following year reveals that both houses spend little time actually doing the countries business. Actual time spent can be found and verified on the web sites of each chamber, www.house.gov and www.senate.gov.

Because congress is in recess, or vacationing, most of the time period between November and January the question as to who governs during this interim period is really more a question of who would be the "caretaker" in place until the new congress is sworn in on January 1. The following is a very viable response:

1. A provisional caretaker committee consisting of the Presidential Cabinet would become the caretaker.

2. Such committee would have NO power to propose or pass new laws.

3. This provisional caretaker committee would only be in office from the date of the retention vote until all newly elected representatives and senators are sworn in on January 1 of the year following the retention vote.

4. No member of the congress voted out of office could be a member of the caretaker committee, if having been appointed to a cabinet position within 180 days of the retention election.

5. Compensation of such committee members would be a 3 month pro-rata amount of the annual salary of the

Speaker of the House of Representatives for the exact time served. Such compensation would be in addition to the salary received as a member of the President's cabinet.

6. The caretaker committee would be required to meet a minimum of once every two weeks to address any governing issues or concerns that may arise. It must remember that this caretaker committee at most would be in session only for approximately 90 days - - not a significant amount of time when compared the total amount of time congress takes off each year.

The United States of America does not have a perfect government. Such a government does not exist. The United States come as close to perfection as has been achieved since King Hammurabi handed down the first written code of laws over 3,700 years ago.

Also realize, no government lasts forever. Witness history. This government, the government of a representative republic may one day perish but it should not perish merely because self serving and corrupted elected representatives have put money and power ahead of the welfare of their constituents. When we read that a senator, 80 plus years of age, who has served 6 terms and contemplates a 7th, or a representative, also 80 plus years of age, has served 24 terms and contemplates that 25^h term, it may be not so much for the desire to serve but rather for the desire to continue wearing the robe of pseudo- aristocracy.

Champion the Every 20 Year solution and help give this country back to those whom it serves. Only the support of each and every American citizen, working with and through their state legislatures, can make this happen. The Founder and Supporters of the Every 20 Year organization implores you to choose wisely and act now, for your sake and that of your children and grandchildren, and all future generations who may never know the county our founding fathers crafted for us.

About the Author and Executive Director of Every 20 Years

Thomas E. McDonald is the Founder and Executive Director of Every 20 Years and established the organization in 2013. You can lend your support by visiting and sharing our website: www.every20years.us.

Tom is also an Adjunct Faculty Professor in the Paralegal Studies Program at Phoenix College, Phoenix, Arizona.

Tom founded Thomas E. McDonald Mediation Services in 2011 and currently provides mediation services in complex contractual matters. You can visit www.thomasemcdonald.com for further information.

Tom's educational background includes:
B.A. Degree from St. Ambrose University, 1972,
Juris Doctorate Degree from Creighton University, 1976,
M.S. Degree from the School of Justice Studies at Arizona State University, 1995.

Tom began his legal career in Iowa City, Iowa in the private practice of law, founding McDonald Law Offices in 1976 and continuing in private practice for 12 years. From 1985 to 1988 Tom served as a Judicial Magistrate Judge in Johnson County, Iowa. Tom resigned from the bench and ended his private practice in the fall of 1988 to attend graduate school at Arizona State University.

Beginning in 1989 Tom began working for the State of Arizona and from 1989 to 2000 held various positions with different state agencies including:

Office of the Attorney General, 1989-1990.

The Arizona Department of Corrections, Legal
Analyst, 1990-1991 and 1993-1994.

Administrative Law Judge, Arizona Department of
Economic Security, 1991 – 1993.

Office of the Attorney General, Managing Attorney.
South Region, Division of Child Support
Enforcement, 1995 – 2000.

In 2000 Tom moved to Ann Arbor, Michigan and assumed the position of Central Regional Director for Development and Membership of Legatus, an international organization for business executives.

Tom is a member in good standing of both the Iowa State Bar and the State Bar of Arizona.

Tom and his wife Mary currently reside in Scottsdale, Arizona.

Acknowledgements

It is impossible for an individual to write a book and truly call it their own. There are so many people that help in so many ways it is difficult, if not impossible to include everyone in any type of acknowledgment. But I shall try.

I must first thank my students that decide to take my classes each semester of each year. I teach in the Paralegal Studies Program at Phoenix College in Phoenix, Arizona. It is my students who, probably unbeknownst to them, give me the drive and desire to continually strive to learn and improve each semester.

It is a result of my continual reading and research, especially in the area of Constitutional Law that I began to formulate the idea that I set forth in this book, and on my website, www.every20years.us. It is an idea that has been festering and growing for several years. I concluded that we, the citizens of this country, need to do something about the way our representatives and senators are elected in this country. I am not the first to ponder this issue, but I decided, thanks to my students, to do something about it. I believe it was Benjamin Franklin, who said, and I am paraphrasing, "Man makes mistakes, but the biggest mistake a man can make is to do nothing." So I decided to do something.

Next I would like to acknowledge my very good friend Phillip Roman who was the primary editor of this endeavor. Phil was the first person I asked to read the first draft of my manuscript which he so willingly and gladly did. With Phil's help and guidance, and expertise I might add, the first draft was followed by subsequent drafts, which I would like to believe each succeeding draft was better than the one it replaced. This was all because of Phil and I thank you Phil. You are a great friend.

Next I would like to acknowledge specifically two of my former students by name. Thank you to Kevin G. Howell and David A. Garcia who took time from their busy lives to read my manuscript and give me valuable and honest feedback.

Lastly, and this should actually say firstly rather than lastly, I want to thank my family. My wife Mary, a teacher, who has been by my side for 45 years and although is not schooled in the law, always looked at whatever I wrote from her background of an elementary and pre-school teacher. As a teacher she looked at sentence structure, punctuation, especially advising me to take out the numerous commas that lawyers so love to use. Thank you, Mary, I love you.

To my daughter Michelle Rooney, my son Matthew McDonald, and my daughter Megan McDonald, thanks for taking the time to read my manuscript. Each of you read a different draft and I think your comments were very biased in that you said each was great, when I am not so sure they were, but then that is what you have done all your lives, as children and as adults, saying the right thing and giving me the confidence to keep going. Thanks guys, I love you.

Lastly, because the previous lastly was not really the final lastly, I want to thank my parents, Alfred and Mary McDonald. I am blessed that both of my parents are still living, in the family home I might add, and are both 92 years of age. I sent them a copy of the original manuscript to let them know what I was undertaking and, after reading it, commented how brilliant their son was. Thanks Mom and Dad, I love you both and I am blessed that you were here for this, as you have been here for me all of my life.

APPENDIX A

THE CONSTITUTION OF THE UNITED STATES OF AMERICA

(Preamble)

We the People of the United States, in Order to form a more perfect Union, establish Justice, insure domestic Tranquility, provide for the common defence (sic), promote the general Welfare, and secure the Blessings of Liberty to ourselves and our Posterity, do ordain and establish this Constitution for the United States of America.

Article I

Section 1

All legislative Powers herein granted shall be vested in a Congress of the United States, which shall consist of a Senate and House of Representatives.

Section 2

1: The House of Representatives shall be composed of Members chosen every second Year by the People of the several States, and the Electors in each State shall have the Qualifications requisite for Electors of the most numerous Branch of the State Legislature.

2: No Person shall be a Representative who shall not have attained to the Age of twenty five Years, and been seven Years a Citizen of the United States, and who shall not, when elected, be an Inhabitant of that State in which he shall be chosen.

3: Representatives and direct Taxes shall be apportioned among the several States which may be included within this Union, according to their respective Numbers, which shall be determined by adding to the whole Number of free Persons, including those bound to Service for a Term of Years, and excluding Indians not taxed, three fifths of all other Persons.[2] The actual Enumeration shall be made within three Years after the first Meeting of the Congress of the United States, and within every subsequent Term of ten Years, in such Manner as they shall by Law direct. The Number of Representatives shall not exceed one for every thirty Thousand, but each State shall have at Least one Representative; and until such enumeration shall be made, the State of New Hampshire shall be entitled to chuse (sic) three, Massachusetts eight, Rhode-Island and Providence Plantations one, Connecticut five, New-York six, New Jersey four, Pennsylvania eight, Delaware one, Maryland six, Virginia ten, North Carolina five, South Carolina five, and Georgia three.

4: When vacancies happen in the Representation from any State, the Executive Authority thereof shall issue Writs of Election to fill such Vacancies.

5: The House of Representatives shall chuse their Speaker and other Officers; and shall have the sole Power of Impeachment.

Section 3

1: The Senate of the United States shall be composed of two Senators from each State, chosen by the Legislature thereof,[3] for six Years; and each Senator shall have one Vote.

2: Immediately after they shall be assembled in Consequence of the first Election, they shall be divided as equally as may be into three Classes. The Seats of the Senators of the first Class shall be vacated at the Expiration of the second Year, of the second Class at the Expiration of the fourth Year, and of the third Class at the Expiration of the sixth Year, so that one third may be chosen every second Year; and if Vacancies happen by Resignation, or otherwise, during the Recess of the Legislature of any State, the Executive thereof may make temporary Appointments until the next Meeting of the Legislature, which shall then fill such Vacancies.[4]

3: No Person shall be a Senator who shall not have attained to the Age of thirty Years, and been nine Years a Citizen of the United States, and who shall not, when elected, be an Inhabitant of that State for which he shall be chosen.

4: The Vice President of the United States shall be President of the Senate, but shall have no Vote, unless they be equally divided.

5: The Senate shall chuse their other Officers, and also a President pro tempore, in the Absence of the Vice President, or when he shall exercise the Office of President of the United States.

6: The Senate shall have the sole Power to try all Impeachments. When sitting for that Purpose, they shall be on Oath or Affirmation. When the President of the United States is tried, the Chief Justice shall preside: And no Person shall be convicted without the Concurrence of two thirds of the Members present.

7: Judgment in Cases of impeachment shall not extend further than to removal from Office, and disqualification to hold and enjoy any Office of honor, Trust or Profit under the United States: but the Party convicted shall nevertheless be liable and subject to Indictment, Trial, Judgment and Punishment, according to Law.

Section 4

1: The Times, Places and Manner of holding Elections for Senators and Representatives, shall be prescribed in each State by the Legislature thereof; but the Congress may at any time by Law make or alter such Regulations, except as to the Places of chusing (sic) Senators.

2: The Congress shall assemble at least once in every Year, and such Meeting shall be on the first Monday in December,[5] unless they shall by Law appoint a different Day.

Section 5

1: Each House shall be the Judge of the Elections, Returns and Qualifications of its own Members, and a Majority of each shall constitute a Quorum to do Business; but a smaller Number may adjourn from day to day, and may be authorized to compel the Attendance of absent Members, in such Manner, and under such Penalties as each House may provide.

2: Each House may determine the Rules of its Proceedings, punish its Members for disorderly Behaviour (sic), and, with the Concurrence of two thirds, expel a Member.

3: Each House shall keep a Journal of its Proceedings, and from time to time publish the same, excepting such Parts as may in their Judgment require Secrecy; and the Yeas and Nays of the Members of either House on any question shall, at the Desire of one fifth of those Present, be entered on the Journal.

4: Neither House, during the Session of Congress, shall, without the Consent of the other, adjourn for more than three days, nor to any other Place than that in which the two Houses shall be sitting.

Section 6

1: The Senators and Representatives shall receive a Compensation for their Services, to be ascertained by Law, and paid out of the Treasury of the United States.[6] They shall in all Cases, except Treason, Felony and Breach of the Peace, be privileged from Arrest during their Attendance at the Session of their respective Houses, and in going to and returning from the same; and for any Speech or Debate in either House, they shall not be questioned in any other Place.

2: No Senator or Representative shall, during the Time for which he was elected, be appointed to any civil Office under the Authority of the United States, which shall have been created, or the Emoluments whereof shall have been encreased during such time; and no Person holding any Office under the United States, shall be a Member of either House during his Continuance in Office.

Section 7

1: All Bills for raising Revenue shall originate in the House of Representatives; but the Senate may propose or concur with Amendments as on other Bills.

2: Every Bill which shall have passed the House of Representatives and the Senate, shall, before it become a Law, be presented to the President of the United States; If he approve he shall sign it, but if not he shall return it, with his Objections to that House in which it shall have originated, who shall enter the Objections at large on their Journal, and proceed to reconsider it. If after such Reconsideration two thirds of that House shall agree to pass the Bill, it shall be sent, together with the Objections, to the other House, by which it shall likewise be reconsidered, and if approved by two thirds of that House, it shall become a Law. But in all such Cases the Votes of both Houses shall be determined by yeas and Nays, and the Names of the Persons voting for and against the Bill shall be entered on the Journal of each House respectively. If any Bill shall not be returned by the President within ten Days (Sundays excepted) after it shall have been presented to him, the Same shall be a Law, in like Manner as if he had signed it, unless the Congress by their Adjournment prevent its Return, in which Case it shall not be a Law.

3: Every Order, Resolution, or Vote to which the Concurrence of the Senate and House of Representatives may be necessary (except on a question of Adjournment) shall be presented to the President of the United States; and before the Same shall take Effect, shall be approved by him, or being disapproved by him, shall be repassed (sic) by two thirds of the Senate and House of Representatives, according to the Rules and Limitations prescribed in the Case of a Bill.

Section 8

1: The Congress shall have Power To lay and collect Taxes, Duties, Imposts and Excises, to pay the Debts and provide for the common Defence and general Welfare of the United States; but all Duties, Imposts and Excises shall be uniform throughout the United States;

2: To borrow Money on the credit of the United States;

3: To regulate Commerce with foreign Nations, and among the several States, and with the Indian Tribes;

4: To establish an uniform Rule of Naturalization, and uniform Laws on the subject of Bankruptcies throughout the United States;

5: To coin Money, regulate the Value thereof, and of foreign Coin, and fix the Standard of Weights and Measures;

6: To provide for the Punishment of counterfeiting the Securities and current Coin of the United States;

7: To establish Post Offices and post Roads;

8: To promote the Progress of Science and useful Arts, by securing for limited Times to Authors and Inventors the exclusive Right to their respective Writings and Discoveries;

9: To constitute Tribunals inferior to the supreme Court;

10: To define and punish Piracies and Felonies committed on the high Seas, and Offences against the Law of Nations;

11: To declare War, grant Letters of Marque and Reprisal, and make Rules concerning Captures on Land and Water;

12: To raise and support Armies, but no Appropriation of Money to that Use shall be for a longer Term than two Years;

13: To provide and maintain a Navy;

14: To make Rules for the Government and Regulation of the land and naval Forces;

15: To provide for calling forth the Militia to execute the Laws of the Union, suppress Insurrections and repel Invasions;

16: To provide for organizing, arming, and disciplining, the Militia, and for governing such Part of them as may be employed in the Service of the United States, reserving to the States respectively, the Appointment of the Officers, and the Authority of training the Militia according to the discipline prescribed by Congress;

17: To exercise exclusive Legislation in all Cases whatsoever, over such District (not exceeding ten Miles square) as may, by Cession of particular States, and the Acceptance of Congress, become the Seat of the Government of the United States, and to exercise like Authority over all Places purchased by the Consent of the Legislature of the State in which the Same shall be, for the Erection of Forts, Magazines, Arsenals, dock-Yards, and other needful Buildings;--And

18: To make all Laws which shall be necessary and proper for carrying into Execution the foregoing Powers, and all other Powers vested by this Constitution in the Government of the United States, or in any Department or Officer thereof.

Section 9

1: The Migration or Importation of such Persons as any of the States now existing shall think proper to admit, shall not be prohibited by the Congress prior to the Year one thousand eight hundred and eight, but a Tax or duty may be imposed on such Importation, not exceeding ten dollars for each Person.

2: The Privilege of the Writ of Habeas Corpus shall not be suspended, unless when in Cases of Rebellion or Invasion the public Safety may require it.

3: No Bill of Attainder or ex post facto Law shall be passed.

4: No Capitation, or other direct, Tax shall be laid, unless in Proportion to the Census or Enumeration herein before directed to be taken.[Z]

5: No Tax or Duty shall be laid on Articles exported from any State.

6: No Preference shall be given by any Regulation of Commerce or Revenue to the Ports of one State over those of another: nor shall Vessels bound to, or from, one State, be obliged to enter, clear, or pay Duties in another.

7: No Money shall be drawn from the Treasury, but in Consequence of Appropriations made by Law; and a regular Statement and Account of the Receipts and Expenditures of all public Money shall be published from time to time.

8: No Title of Nobility shall be granted by the United States: And no Person holding any Office of Profit or Trust under them, shall, without the Consent of the Congress, accept of any present, Emolument, Office, or Title, of any kind whatever, from any King, Prince, or foreign State.

Section 10

1: No State shall enter into any Treaty, Alliance, or Confederation; grant Letters of Marque and Reprisal; coin Money; emit Bills of Credit; make any Thing but gold and silver Coin a Tender in Payment of Debts; pass any Bill of Attainder, ex post facto Law, or Law impairing the Obligation of Contracts, or grant any Title of Nobility.

2: No State shall, without the Consent of the Congress, lay any Imposts or Duties on Imports or Exports, except what may be absolutely necessary for executing it's inspection Laws: and the net Produce of all Duties and Imposts, laid by any State on Imports or Exports, shall be for the Use of the Treasury of the United States; and all such Laws shall be subject to the Revision and Controul (sic) of the Congress.

3: No State shall, without the Consent of Congress, lay any Duty of Tonnage, keep Troops, or Ships of War in time of Peace, enter into any Agreement or Compact with another State, or with a foreign Power, or engage in War, unless actually invaded, or in such imminent Danger as will not admit of delay.

Article II

Section 1

1: The executive Power shall be vested in a President of the United States of America. He shall hold his Office during the Term of four Years, and, together with the Vice President, chosen for the same Term, be elected, as follows

2: Each State shall appoint, in such Manner as the Legislature thereof may direct, a Number of Electors, equal to the whole Number of Senators and Representatives to which the State may be entitled in the Congress: but no Senator or Representative, or Person holding an Office of Trust or Profit under the United States, shall be appointed an Elector.

3: The Electors shall meet in their respective States, and vote by Ballot for two Persons, of whom one at least shall not be an Inhabitant of the same State with themselves. And they shall make a List of all the Persons voted for, and of the Number of Votes for each; which List they shall sign and certify, and transmit sealed to the Seat of the Government of the United States, directed to the President of the Senate. The President of the Senate shall, in the Presence of the Senate and House of Representatives, open all the Certificates, and the Votes shall then be counted. The Person having the greatest Number of Votes shall be the President, if such Number be a Majority of the whole Number of Electors appointed; and if there be more than one who have such Majority, and have an equal Number of Votes, then the House of Representatives shall immediately chuse by Ballot one of them for President; and if no Person have a Majority, then from the five highest on the List the said House shall in like Manner chuse the President. But in chusing the President, the Votes shall be taken by States, the Representation from each State having one Vote; A quorum for this Purpose shall consist of a Member or Members from two thirds of the States, and a Majority of all the States shall be necessary to a Choice. In every Case, after the Choice of the President, the Person having the greatest Number of Votes of the Electors shall be the Vice President. But if there should remain two or more who have equal Votes, the Senate shall chuse from them by Ballot the Vice President.[8]

4: The Congress may determine the Time of chusing the Electors, and the Day on which they shall give their Votes; which Day shall be the same throughout the United States.

5: No Person except a natural born Citizen, or a Citizen of the United States, at the time of the Adoption of this Constitution, shall be eligible to the Office of President; neither shall any Person be eligible to that Office who shall not have attained to the Age of thirty five Years, and been fourteen Years a Resident within the United States.

6: In Case of the Removal of the President from Office, or of his Death, Resignation, or Inability to discharge the Powers and Duties of the said Office,[9] the Same shall devolve on the Vice President, and the Congress may by Law provide for the Case of Removal, Death, Resignation or Inability, both of the President and Vice President, declaring what Officer shall then act as President, and such Officer shall act accordingly, until the Disability be removed, or a President shall be elected.

7: The President shall, at stated Times, receive for his Services, a Compensation, which shall neither be increased nor diminished during the Period for which he shall have been elected, and he shall not receive within that Period any other Emolument from the United States, or any of them.

8: Before he enter on the Execution of his Office, he shall take the following Oath or Affirmation:--"I do solemnly swear (or affirm) that I will faithfully execute the Office of President of the United States, and will to the best of my Ability, preserve, protect and defend the Constitution of the United States."

Section 2

1: The President shall be Commander in Chief of the Army and Navy of the United States, and of the Militia of the several States, when called into the actual Service of the United States; he may require the Opinion, in writing, of the principal Officer in each of the executive Departments, upon any Subject relating to the Duties of their respective Offices, and he shall have Power to grant Reprieves and Pardons for Offences against the United States, except in Cases of Impeachment.

2: He shall have Power, by and with the Advice and Consent of the Senate, to make Treaties, provided two thirds of the Senators present concur; and he shall nominate, and by and with the Advice and Consent of the Senate, shall appoint Ambassadors, other public Ministers and Consuls, Judges of the supreme Court, and all other Officers of the United States, whose Appointments are not herein otherwise provided for, and which shall be established by Law: but the Congress may by Law vest the Appointment of such inferior Officers, as they think proper, in the President alone, in the Courts of Law, or in the Heads of Departments.

3: The President shall have Power to fill up all Vacancies that may happen during the Recess of the Senate, by granting Commissions which shall expire at the End of their next Session.

Section 3

He shall from time to time give to the Congress Information of the State of the Union, and recommend to their Consideration such Measures as he shall judge necessary and expedient; he may, on extraordinary

Occasions, convene both Houses, or either of them, and in Case of Disagreement between them, with Respect to the Time of Adjournment, he may adjourn them to such Time as he shall think proper; he shall receive Ambassadors and other public Ministers; he shall take Care that the Laws be faithfully executed, and shall Commission all the Officers of the United States.

Section 4

The President, Vice President and all civil Officers of the United States, shall be removed from Office on Impeachment for, and Conviction of, Treason, Bribery, or other high Crimes and Misdemeanors.

Article III

Section 1

The judicial Power of the United States, shall be vested in one supreme Court, and in such inferior Courts as the Congress may from time to time ordain and establish. The Judges, both of the supreme and inferior Courts, shall hold their Offices during good Behaviour, and shall, at stated Times, receive for their Services, a Compensation, which shall not be diminished during their Continuance in Office.

Section 2

1: The judicial Power shall extend to all Cases, in Law and Equity, arising under this Constitution, the Laws of the United States, and Treaties made, or which shall be made, under their Authority;--to all Cases affecting Ambassadors, other public Ministers and Consuls;--to all Cases of admiralty and maritime Jurisdiction;--to Controversies to which the United States shall be a Party;--to Controversies between two or more States;--between a State and Citizens of another State;[10] -- between Citizens of different States, --between Citizens of the same State claiming Lands under Grants of different States, and between a State, or the Citizens thereof, and foreign States, Citizens or Subjects.

2: In all Cases affecting Ambassadors, other public Ministers and Consuls, and those in which a State shall be Party, the supreme Court shall have original Jurisdiction. In all the other Cases before mentioned, the supreme Court shall have appellate Jurisdiction, both as to Law and Fact, with such Exceptions, and under such Regulations as the Congress shall make.

3: The Trial of all Crimes, except in Cases of Impeachment, shall be by Jury; and such Trial shall be held in the State where the said Crimes shall have been committed; but when not committed within any State, the Trial shall be at such Place or Places as the Congress may by Law have directed.

Section 3

1: Treason against the United States, shall consist only in levying War against them, or in adhering to their Enemies, giving them Aid and Comfort. No Person shall be convicted of Treason unless on the Testimony of two Witnesses to the same overt Act, or on Confession in open Court.

2: The Congress shall have Power to declare the Punishment of Treason, but no Attainder of Treason shall work Corruption of Blood, or Forfeiture except during the Life of the Person attainted.

Article IV

Section 1

Full Faith and Credit shall be given in each State to the public Acts, Records, and judicial Proceedings of every other State. And the Congress may by general Laws prescribe the Manner in which such Acts, Records and Proceedings shall be proved, and the Effect thereof.

Section 2

1: The Citizens of each State shall be entitled to all Privileges and Immunities of Citizens in the several States.

2: A Person charged in any State with Treason, Felony, or other Crime, who shall flee from Justice, and be found in another State, shall on Demand of the executive Authority of the State from which he fled, be delivered up, to be removed to the State having Jurisdiction of the Crime.

3: No Person held to Service or Labour (sic) in one State, under the Laws thereof, escaping into another, shall, in Consequence of any Law or Regulation therein, be discharged from such Service or Labour, but shall be delivered up on Claim of the Party to whom such Service or Labour may be due.

Section 3

1: New States may be admitted by the Congress into this Union; but no new State shall be formed or erected within the Jurisdiction of any other State; nor any State be formed by the Junction of two or more States, or Parts of States, without the Consent of the Legislatures of the States concerned as well as of the Congress.

2: The Congress shall have Power to dispose of and make all needful Rules and Regulations respecting the Territory or other Property belonging to the United States; and nothing in this Constitution shall be so construed as to Prejudice any Claims of the United States, or of any particular State.

Section 4

The United States shall guarantee to every State in this Union a Republican Form of Government, and shall protect each of them against Invasion; and on Application of the Legislature, or of the Executive (when the Legislature cannot be convened) against domestic Violence.

Article V

The Congress, whenever two thirds of both Houses shall deem it necessary, shall propose Amendments to this Constitution, or, on the Application of the Legislatures of two thirds of the several States, shall call a Convention for proposing Amendments, which, in either Case, shall be valid to all Intents and Purposes, as Part of this Constitution, when ratified by the Legislatures of three fourths of the several States, or by Conventions in three fourths thereof, as the one or the other Mode of Ratification may be proposed by the Congress; Provided that no Amendment which may be made prior to the Year One thousand eight hundred and eight shall in any Manner affect the first and fourth Clauses in the Ninth Section of the first Article; and that no State, without its Consent, shall be deprived of its equal Suffrage in the Senate.

Article VI

1: All Debts contracted and Engagements entered into, before the Adoption of this Constitution, shall be as valid against the United States under this Constitution, as under the Confederation.

2: This Constitution, and the Laws of the United States which shall be made in Pursuance thereof; and all Treaties made, or which shall be made, under the Authority of the United States, shall be the supreme Law of the Land; and the Judges in every State shall be bound thereby, any Thing in the Constitution or Laws of any State to the Contrary notwithstanding.

3: The Senators and Representatives before mentioned, and the Members of the several State Legislatures, and all executive and judicial Officers, both of the United States and of the several States, shall be bound by Oath or Affirmation, to support this Constitution; but no religious Test shall ever be required as a Qualification to any Office or public Trust under the United States.

Article VII

The Ratification of the Conventions of nine States, shall be sufficient for the Establishment of this Constitution between the States so ratifying the Same.

Amendment I (1791)

Congress shall make no law respecting an establishment of religion, or prohibiting the free exercise thereof; or abridging the freedom of speech, or of the press; or the right of the people peaceably to assemble, and to petition the Government for a redress of grievances.

Amendment II (1791)

A well regulated Militia, being necessary to the security of a free State, the right of the people to keep and bear Arms, shall not be infringed.

Amendment III (1791)

No Soldier shall, in time of peace be quartered in any house, without the consent of the Owner, nor in time of war, but in a manner to be prescribed by law.

Amendment IV (1791)

The right of the people to be secure in their persons, houses, papers, and effects, against unreasonable searches and seizures, shall not be violated, and no Warrants shall issue, but upon probable cause, supported by Oath or affirmation, and particularly describing the place to be searched, and the persons or things to be seized.

Amendment V (1791)

No person shall be held to answer for a capital, or otherwise infamous crime, unless on a presentment or indictment of a Grand Jury, except in cases arising in the land or naval forces, or in the Militia, when in actual service in time of War or public danger; nor shall any person be subject for the same offence to be twice put in jeopardy of life or limb; nor shall be compelled in any criminal case to be a witness against himself, nor be deprived of life, liberty, or property, without due process of law; nor shall private property be taken for public use, without just compensation.

Amendment VI (1791)

In all criminal prosecutions, the accused shall enjoy the right to a speedy and public trial, by an impartial jury of the State and district wherein the crime shall have been committed, which district shall have been previously ascertained by law, and to be informed of the nature and cause of the accusation; to be confronted with the witnesses against him; to have compulsory process for obtaining witnesses in his favor, and to have the Assistance of Counsel for his defence.

Amendment VII (1791)

In Suits at common law, where the value in controversy shall exceed twenty dollars, the right of trial by jury shall be preserved, and no fact tried by a jury, shall be otherwise re-examined in any Court of the United States, than according to the rules of the common law.

Amendment VIII (1791)

Excessive bail shall not be required, nor excessive fines imposed, nor cruel and unusual punishments inflicted.

Amendment IX (1791)

The enumeration in the Constitution, of certain rights, shall not be construed to deny or disparage others retained by the people. Amendment

Amendment X (1791)

The powers not delegated to the United States by the Constitution, nor prohibited by it to the States, are reserved to the States respectively, or to the people.

Amendment XI (1798)

The Judicial power of the United States shall not be construed to extend to any suit in law or equity, commenced or prosecuted against one of the United States by Citizens of another State, or by Citizens or Subjects of any Foreign State.

Amendment XII (1804)

The Electors shall meet in their respective states and vote by ballot for President and Vice-President, one of whom, at least, shall not be an inhabitant of the same state with themselves; they shall name in their ballots the person voted for as President, and in distinct ballots the person voted for as Vice-President, and they shall make distinct lists of all persons voted for as President, and of all persons voted for as Vice-President, and of the number of votes for each, which lists they shall sign and certify, and transmit sealed to the seat of the government of the United States, directed to the President of the Senate;—The President of the Senate shall, in the presence of the Senate and House of Representatives, open all the certificates and the votes shall then be counted;—The person having the greatest Number of votes for President, shall be the President, if such number be a majority of the whole number of Electors appointed; and if no person have such majority, then from the persons having the highest numbers not exceeding three on the list of those voted for as President, the House of Representatives shall choose immediately, by ballot, the President. But in choosing the President, the votes shall be taken by states, the representation from each state having one vote; a quorum for this purpose shall consist of a member or members from two-thirds of the states, and a majority of all the states shall be necessary to a choice. And if the House of Representatives shall not choose a President whenever the right of choice shall devolve upon them, before the fourth day of March next following, then the Vice-President shall act as President, as in the case of the death or other constitutional disability of the President—The person having the greatest number of votes as Vice-President, shall be the Vice-President, if such number be a majority of the whole number of Electors appointed, and if no person have a majority, then from the two highest numbers on the list, the Senate shall choose the Vice-President; a quorum for the purpose shall consist of two-thirds of the whole number of Senators, and a majority of the whole number shall be necessary to a choice. But no person constitutionally ineligible to the office of President shall be eligible to that of Vice-President of the United States.

Amendment XIII (1865)

Section 1. Neither slavery nor involuntary servitude, except as a punishment for crime whereof the party shall have been duly convicted, shall exist within the United States, or any place subject to their jurisdiction.

Section 2. Congress shall have power to enforce this article by appropriate legislation.

Amendment XIV (1868)

Section 1. All persons born or naturalized in the United States and subject to the jurisdiction thereof, are citizens of the United States and of the State wherein they reside. No State shall make or enforce any law which shall abridge the privileges or immunities of citizens of the United States; nor shall any State deprive any person of life, liberty, or property, without due process of law; nor deny to any person within its jurisdiction the equal protection of the laws.

Section 2. Representatives shall be apportioned among the several States according to their respective numbers, counting the whole number of persons in each State, excluding Indians not taxed. But when the right to vote at any election for the choice of electors for President and Vice President of the United States, Representatives in Congress, the Executive and Judicial officers of a State, or the members of the Legislature thereof, is denied to any of the male inhabitants of such State, being twenty-one years of age, and citizens of the United States, or in any way abridged, except for participation in rebellion, or other crime, the basis of representation therein shall be reduced in the proportion which the number of such male citizens shall bear to the whole number of male citizens twenty-one years of age in such State.

Section 3. No person shall be a Senator or Representative in Congress, or elector of President and Vice President, or hold any office, civil or military, under the United States, or under any State, who, having previously taken an oath, as a member of Congress, or as an officer of the United States, or as a member of any State legislature, or as an executive or judicial officer of any State, to support the Constitution of the United States, shall have engaged in insurrection or rebellion against the same, or given aid or comfort to the enemies thereof. But Congress may by a vote of two-thirds of each House, remove such disability.

Section 4. The validity of the public debt of the United States, authorized by law, including debts incurred for payment of pensions and bounties for services in suppressing insurrection or rebellion, shall not be questioned. But neither the United States nor any State shall assume or pay any debt or obligation incurred in aid of insurrection or rebellion against the United States, or any claim for the loss or emancipation of any slave; but all such debts, obligations and claims shall be held illegal and void.

Section 5. The Congress shall have power to enforce, by appropriate legislation, the provisions of this article.

Amendment XV (1870)

Section 1. The right of citizens of the United States to vote shall not be denied or abridged by the United States or by any State on account of race, color, or previous condition of servitude.

Section 2. The Congress shall have power to enforce this article by appropriate legislation.

Amendment XVI (1913)

The Congress shall have power to lay and collect taxes on incomes, from whatever source derived, without apportionment among the several States, and without regard to any census or enumeration.

Amendment XVII (1913)

The Senate of the United States shall be composed of two Senators from each State, elected by the people thereof, for six years; and each Senator shall have one vote. The electors in each State shall have the qualifications requisite for electors of the most numerous branch of the State legislatures.

When vacancies happen in the representation of any State in the Senate, the executive authority of such State shall issue writs of election to fill such vacancies: Provided, That the legislature of any State may empower the executive thereof to make temporary appointments until the people fill the vacancies by election as the legislature may direct.

This amendment shall not be so construed as to affect the election or term of any Senator chosen before it becomes valid as part of the Constitution.

Amendment XVIII (1919)

Section 1. After one year from the ratification of this article the manufacture, sale, or transportation of intoxicating liquors within, the importation thereof into, or the exportation thereof from the United States and all territory subject to the jurisdiction thereof for beverage purposes is hereby prohibited.

Section 2. The Congress and the several States shall have concurrent power to enforce this article by appropriate legislation.

Section 3. This article shall be inoperative unless it shall have been ratified as an amendment to the Constitution by the legislatures of the several States, as provided in the Constitution, within seven years from the date of the submission hereof to the States by the Congress.

Amendment XIX (1920)

The right of citizens of the United States to vote shall not be denied or abridged by the United States or by any State on account of sex.

Congress shall have power to enforce this article by appropriate legislation.

Amendment XX (1933)

Section 1. The terms of the President and Vice President shall end at noon on the 20th day of January, and the terms of Senators and Representatives at noon on the 3d day of January, of the years in which such terms would have ended if this article had not been ratified; and the terms of their successors shall then begin.

Section 2. The Congress shall assemble at least once in every year, and such meeting shall begin at noon on the 3d day of January, unless they shall by law appoint a different day.

Section 3. If, at the time fixed for the beginning of the term of the President, the President elect shall have died, the Vice President elect shall become President. If a President shall not have been chosen before the time fixed for the beginning of his term, or if the President elect shall have failed to qualify, then the Vice President elect shall act as President until a President shall have qualified; and the Congress may by law provide for the case wherein neither a President elect nor a Vice President elect shall have qualified, declaring who shall then act as President, or the manner in which one who is to act shall be selected, and such person shall act accordingly until a President or Vice President shall have qualified.

Section 4. The Congress may by law provide for the case of the death of any of the persons from whom the House of Representatives may choose a President whenever the right of choice shall have devolved upon them, and for the case of the death of any of the persons from whom the Senate may choose a Vice President whenever the right of choice shall have devolved upon them.

Section 5. Sections 1 and 2 shall take effect on the 15th day of October following the ratification of this article.

Section 6. This article shall be inoperative unless it shall have been ratified as an amendment to the Constitution by the legislatures of three-fourths of the several States within seven years from the date of its submission.

Amendment XXI (1933)

Section 1. The eighteenth article of amendment to the Constitution of the United States is hereby repealed.

Section 2. The transportation or importation into any State, Territory, or possession of the United States for delivery or use therein of intoxicating liquors, in violation of the laws thereof, is hereby prohibited.

Section 3. This article shall be inoperative unless it shall have been ratified as an amendment to the Constitution by conventions in the several States, as provided in the Constitution, within seven years from the date of the submission hereof to the States by the Congress.

Amendment XXII (1951)

Section 1. No person shall be elected to the office of the President more than twice, and no person who has held the office of President, or acted as President, for more than two years of a term to which some other person was elected President shall be elected to the office of the President more than once. But this Article shall not apply to any person holding the office of President, when this Article was proposed by the Congress, and shall not prevent any person who may be holding the office of President, or acting as President, during the term within which this Article becomes operative from holding the office of President or acting as President during the remainder of such term.

Section 2. This article shall be inoperative unless it shall have been ratified as an amendment to the Constitution by the legislatures of three-fourths of the several States within seven years from the date of its submission to the States by the Congress.

Amendment XXIII (1961)

Section 1. The District constituting the seat of Government of the United States shall appoint in such manner as the Congress may direct:

A number of electors of President and Vice President equal to the whole number of Senators and Representatives in Congress to which the District would be entitled if it were a State, but in no event more than the least populous State; they shall be in addition to those appointed by the States, but they shall be considered, for the purposes of the election of President and Vice President, to be electors appointed by a State; and they shall meet in the District and perform such duties as provided by the twelfth article of amendment.

Section 2. The Congress shall have power to enforce this article by appropriate legislation.

Amendment XXIV (1964)

Section 1. The right of citizens of the United States to vote in any primary or other election for President or Vice President for electors for President or Vice President, or for Senator or Representative in Congress, shall not be denied or abridged by the United States or any State by reason of failure to pay any poll tax or other tax.

Section 2. The Congress shall have power to enforce this article by appropriate legislation.

Amendment XXV (1967)

Section 1. In case of the removal of the President from office or of his death or resignation, the Vice President shall become President.

Section 2. Whenever there is a vacancy in the office of the Vice President, the President shall nominate a Vice President who shall take office upon confirmation by a majority vote of both Houses of Congress.

Section 3. Whenever the President transmits to the President pro tempore of the Senate and the Speaker of the House of Representatives his written declaration that he is unable to discharge the powers and duties of his office, and until he transmits to them a written declaration to the contrary, such powers and duties shall be discharged by the Vice President as Acting President.

Section 4. Whenever the Vice President and a majority of either the principal officers of the executive departments or of such other body as Congress may by law provide, transmit to the President pro tempore of the Senate and the Speaker of the House of Representatives their written declaration that the President is unable to discharge the powers and duties of his office, the Vice President shall immediately assume the powers and duties of the office as Acting President.

Thereafter, when the President transmits to the President pro tempore of the Senate and the Speaker of the House of Representatives his written declaration that no inability exists, he shall resume the powers and duties of his office unless the Vice President and a majority of either the principal officers of the executive department or of such other body as

Congress may by law provide, transmit within four days to the President pro tempore of the Senate and the Speaker of the House of Representatives their written declaration that the President is unable to discharge the powers and duties of his office. Thereupon Congress shall decide the issue, assembling within forty-eight hours for that purpose if not in session. If the Congress, within twenty-one days after receipt of the latter written declaration, or, if Congress is not in session, within twenty-one days after Congress is required to assemble, determines by two-thirds vote of both Houses that the President is unable to discharge the powers and duties of his office, the Vice President shall continue to discharge the same as Acting President; otherwise, the President shall resume the powers and duties of his office.

Amendment XXVI (1971)

Section 1. The right of citizens of the United States, who are eighteen years of age or older, to vote shall not be denied or abridged by the United States or by any State on account of age.

Section 2. The Congress shall have power to enforce this article by appropriate legislation.

Amendment XXVII (1992)

No law varying the compensation for the services of the Senators and Representatives shall take effect, until an election of Representatives shall have intervened.

Thomas Jefferson, First Inaugural Address, March 4, 1801

CALLED upon to undertake the duties of the first executive office of our country, I avail myself of the presence of that portion of my fellow-citizens which is here assembled to express my grateful thanks for the favor with which they have been pleased to look toward me, to declare a sincere consciousness that the task is above my talents, and that I approach it with those anxious and awful presentiments which the greatness of the charge and the weakness of my powers so justly inspire. A rising nation, spread over a wide and fruitful land, traversing all the seas with the rich productions of their industry, engaged in commerce with nations who feel power and forget right, advancing rapidly to destinies beyond the reach of mortal eye—when I contemplate these transcendent objects, and see the honor, the happiness, and the hopes of this beloved country committed to the issue, and the auspices of this day, I shrink from the contemplation, and humble myself before the magnitude of the undertaking. Utterly, indeed, should I despair did not the presence of many whom I here see remind me that in the other high authorities provided by our Constitution I shall find resources of wisdom, of virtue, and of zeal on which to rely under all difficulties. To you, then, gentlemen, who are charged with the sovereign functions of legislation, and to those associated with you, I look with encouragement for that guidance and support which may enable us to steer with safety the vessel in which we are all embarked amidst the conflicting elements of a troubled world

During the contest of opinion through which we have passed the animation of discussions and of exertions has sometimes worn an aspect which might impose on strangers unused to think freely and to speak and to write what they think; but this being now decided by the voice of the nation, announced according to the rules of the Constitution, all will, of course, arrange themselves under the will of the law, and unite in common efforts for the common good. All, too, will bear in mind this sacred principle, that though the will of the majority is in all cases to prevail, that will to be rightful must be reasonable; that the minority possess their equal rights, which equal law must protect, and to violate would be oppression. Let us, then, fellow-citizens, unite with one heart and one mind. Let us restore to social intercourse that harmony and affection without which liberty and even life itself are but dreary things. And let us reflect that, having banished from our land that religious intolerance under which mankind so long bled and suffered, we have yet gained little if we countenance a political intolerance as despotic, as wicked, and capable of as bitter and bloody persecutions. During the throes and convulsions of the ancient world, during the agonizing spasms of infuriated man, seeking through blood and slaughter his long-lost liberty, it was not wonderful that the agitation of the billows should reach even this distant and peaceful shore; that this should be more felt and feared by some and less by others, and should divide opinions as to measures of safety. But every difference of opinion is not a difference of principle. We have called by different names brethren of the same principle. We are all Republicans, we are all Federalists. If there be any among us who would wish to dissolve this Union or to change its republican form, let them stand undisturbed as monuments of the safety with which error of opinion may be tolerated where reason is left free to combat it. I know, indeed, that some honest men fear that a republican government can not (sic) be strong, that this Government is not strong enough; but would the honest patriot, in the full tide of successful experiment, abandon a government which has so far kept us free and firm on the theoretic and visionary fear that this Government, the world's best hope, may by possibility want energy to preserve itself? I trust not. I believe this, on the contrary, the strongest Government on earth. I believe it the only one where every man, at the call of the law, would fly to the standard of the law, and would meet invasions of the public order as his own personal concern. **Sometimes it is said that man can not (sic) be trusted with the government of himself. Can he, then, be trusted with the government of others?** Or have we found angels in the forms of kings to govern him? Let history answer this question.

Let us, then, with courage and confidence pursue our own Federal and Republican principles, our attachment to union and representative government. Kindly separated by nature and a wide ocean from the exterminating havoc of one quarter of the globe; too high-minded to endure the degradations of the others; possessing a chosen country, with room enough for our descendants to the thousandth and thousandth generation; entertaining a due sense of our equal right to the use of our own faculties, to the acquisitions of our own industry, to honor and confidence from our fellow-citizens, resulting not from birth, but from our actions and their sense of them; enlightened by a benign religion, professed, indeed, and practiced in various forms, yet all of them inculcating honesty, truth, temperance, gratitude, and the love of man; acknowledging and adoring an overruling Providence, which by all its dispensations proves that it delights in the happiness of man here and his greater happiness hereafter—with all these blessings, what more is necessary to make us a happy and a prosperous people? Still one thing more, fellow-citizens—a wise and frugal Government, which shall restrain men from injuring one another, shall leave them otherwise free to regulate their own pursuits of industry and improvement, and shall not take from the mouth of labor the bread it has earned. This is the sum of good government, and this is necessary to close the circle of our felicities.

About to enter, fellow-citizens, on the exercise of duties which comprehend everything dear and valuable to you, it is proper you should understand what I deem the essential principles of our Government, and consequently those which ought to shape its Administration. I will compress them within the narrowest compass they will bear, stating the general principle, but not all its limitations. Equal and exact justice to all men, of whatever state or persuasion, religious or political; peace, commerce, and honest friendship with all nations, entangling alliances with none; the support of the State governments in all their rights, as the most competent administrations for our domestic concerns and the surest bulwarks against antirepublican (sic) tendencies; the preservation of the General Government in its whole constitutional vigor, as the sheet anchor of our peace at home and safety abroad; a jealous care of the right of election by the people—a mild and safe corrective of abuses which are lopped by the sword of revolution where peaceable remedies are unprovided (sic); absolute acquiescence in the decisions of the majority, the vital principle of republics, from which is no appeal but to force, the vital principle and immediate parent of despotism; a well disciplined militia, our best reliance in peace and for the first moments of war, till regulars may relieve them; the supremacy of the civil over the military authority; economy in the public expense, that labor may be lightly burthened (sic); the honest payment of our debts and sacred preservation of the public faith; encouragement of agriculture, and of commerce as its handmaid; the diffusion of information and arraignment of all abuses at the bar of the public reason; freedom of religion; freedom of the press, and freedom of person under the protection of the habeas corpus, and trial by juries impartially selected. These principles form the bright constellation which has gone before us and guided our steps through an age of revolution and reformation. The wisdom of our sages and blood of our heroes have been devoted to their attainment. They should be the creed of our political faith, the text of civic instruction, the touchstone by which to try the services of those we trust; and should we wander from them in moments of error or of alarm, let us hasten to retrace our steps and to regain the road which alone leads to peace, liberty, and safety.

I repair, then, fellow-citizens, to the post you have assigned me. With experience enough in subordinate offices to have seen the difficulties of this the greatest of all, I have learnt to expect that it will rarely fall to the lot of imperfect man to retire from this station with the reputation and the favor which bring him into it. Without pretensions to that high confidence you reposed in our first and greatest revolutionary character, whose preeminent services had entitled him to the first place in his country's love and destined for him the fairest page in the volume of faithful history, I ask so much confidence only as may give firmness and effect to the legal administration of your affairs. I shall often go wrong through defect of judgment. When right, I shall often be thought wrong by those whose positions will not command a view of the whole ground. I ask your indulgence for my own errors, which will never be intentional, and your support against the errors of others, who may condemn what they would not if seen in all its parts. The approbation implied by your suffrage is a great consolation to me for the past, and my future solicitude will be to retain the good opinion of those who have bestowed it in advance, to conciliate that of others by doing them all the good in my power, and to be instrumental to the happiness and freedom of all.

Relying, then, on the patronage of your good will, I advance with obedience to the work, ready to retire from it whenever you become sensible how much better choice it is in your power to make. And may that Infinite Power which rules the destinies of the universe lead our councils to what is best, and give them a favorable issue for your peace and prosperity.

APPENDIX C

From Thomas Jefferson to Edward Rutledge, 18 July 1788

To Edward Rutledge

Paris July 18. 1788.

MY DEAR SIR

Messieurs Berard were (sic)to have given me a particular account of the proceeds of the shipments of rice made to them. But they have failed. I fear, from what they mentioned, that the price has been less advantageous than usual, which is unlucky as it falls on the first essay. If on the whole however you get as much, as you would have done by a sale on the spot, it should encourage other adventures, because the price at Havre or Rouen is commonly higher, and because I think you may by trials find out the way to avail yourselves of the Paris retail price. The Carolina rice sold at Paris is separated into three kinds, 1. the whole grains, 2. the broken grains, 3. the small stuff and sell at 10. ₶ 8. ₶ and 6. ₶ the French pound, retail. The whole grains which constitute the 1st. quality are picked out by hand. I would not recommend this operation to be done with you, because labour (sic) is dearer there than here. But I mention these prices to shew (sic) that after making a reasonable deduction for sorting, and leaving a reasonable profit to the retailer, there should still remain a great wholesale price. I shall wish to know from you how much your cargo of rice shipped to Berard netts (sic) you, and how much it would have netted *in hard money* if you had sold it at home.

You promise, in your letter of Octob. 23. 1787. to give me in your next, at large, the <u>conjectures of your Philosopher</u> on the descent of the Creek Indians from the Carthaginians, supposed to have been separated from Hanno's fleet during his periplus (sic). I shall be very glad to receive them, and see nothing impossible in his conjecture. I am glad he means to appeal to the similarity of language, which I consider as the strongest kind of proof it is possible to adduce. I have somewhere read that the language of the ancient Carthaginians is still spoken by their descendants inhabiting the mountainous interior parts of Barbary to which they were obliged to retire by the conquering Arabs. If so, a vocabulary of their tongue can still be got, and if your friend will get one of the Creek language, the comparison will decide. He probably may have made progress in this business: but if he wishes any enquiries to be made on this side the Atlantic, I offer him my services chearfully (sic), my wish being, like his, to ascertain the history of the American aborigines.

I congratulate you on the accession of your state to the new federal constitution. This is the last I have yet heard of, but I expect daily that my own has followed the good example, and suppose it to be already established. Our government wanted bracing. Still we must take care not to run from one extreme to another; not to brace too high. I own I join those in opinion who think a bill of rights necessary. **I apprehend too that the total abandonment of the principle of rotation in the offices of President and Senator will end in abuse. But my confidence is that there will for a long time be virtue and good sense enough in our countrymen to correct abuses** (emphasis added). We can surely boast of having set the world a beautiful example of a government reformed by reason alone without bloodshed. But the world is too far oppressed to profit of the example. On this side the Atlantic the blood of the people is become an inheritance, and those who fatten on it, will not relinquish it easily. The struggle in this country is as yet of doubtful issue. It is in fact between the monarchy, and the parliaments. The nation is no otherwise concerned but as both parties may be induced to let go some of its abuses to court the public favor. The danger is that the people, decieved (sic) by a false cry of liberty may be led to take side with one party, and thus give the other a pretext for crushing them still more. If they can avoid the appeal to arms, the nation will be sure to gain much by this controversy. But if that appeal is made it will depend entirely on the dispositions of the army whether it issue in liberty or despotism. Those dispositions are not as yet known. In the mean time there is great probability that the war kindled in the east will spread from nation to nation and in the long run become general. It began between the Turks and Russians. Then the Emperor entered into it, now the Swedes have taken side, and so probably it will go on from one to another. This country is in a desperate condition to meet a war. The only hope is that England will be as little able to get money, and that a bankruptcy will follow the declaration of war. They first excited the Turks to begin, and now have engaged the Swedes to enter into it. Whether they may not repent it however may well be doubted, and that they may repent it is the hearty prayer of him who has the honour (sic) to be with the most sincere esteem & attachment, my dear Sir Your friend & servt (sic),

TH: JEFFERSON

APPENDIX D

Contract With America, 1994

As Republican Members of the House of Representatives and as citizens seeking to join that body we propose not just to change its policies, but even more important, to restore the bonds of trust between the people and their elected representatives. That is why, in this era of official evasion and posturing, we offer instead a detailed agenda for national renewal, a written commitment with no fine print.

This year's election offers the chance, after four decades of one-party control, to bring to the House a new majority that will transform the way Congress works. That historic change would be the end of government that is too big, too intrusive, and too easy with the public's money. It can be the beginning of a Congress that respects the values and shares the faith of the American family.

Like Lincoln, our first Republican president, we intend to act "with firmness in the right, as God gives us to see the right." To restore accountability to Congress. To end its cycle of scandal and disgrace. To make us all proud again of the way free people govern themselves.

On the first day of the 104th Congress, the new Republican majority will immediately pass the following major reforms, aimed at restoring the faith and trust of the American people in their government:

- FIRST, require all laws that apply to the rest of the country also apply equally to the Congress;
- SECOND, select a major, independent auditing firm to conduct a comprehensive audit of Congress for waste, fraud or abuse;
- THIRD, cut the number of House committees, and cut committee staff by one-third;
- FOURTH, limit the terms of all committee chairs;
- FIFTH, ban the casting of proxy votes in committee;
- SIXTH, require committee meetings to be open to the public;
- SEVENTH, require a three-fifths majority vote to pass a tax increase;
- EIGHTH, guarantee an honest accounting of our Federal Budget by implementing zero base-line budgeting.

Thereafter, within the first 100 days of the 104th Congress, we shall bring to the House Floor the following bills, each to be given full and open debate, each to be given a clear and fair vote and each to be immediately available this day for public inspection and scrutiny.

1. THE FISCAL RESPONSIBILITY ACT: A balanced budget/tax limitation amendment and a legislative line-item veto to restore fiscal responsibility to an out- of-control Congress, requiring them to live under the same budget constraints as families and businesses.

2. THE TAKING BACK OUR STREETS ACT: An anti-crime package including stronger truth-in- sentencing, "good faith" exclusionary rule exemptions, effective death penalty provisions, and cuts in social spending from this summer's "crime" bill to fund prison construction and additional law enforcement to keep people secure in their neighborhoods and kids safe in their schools.

3. THE PERSONAL RESPONSIBILITY ACT:
Discourage illegitimacy and teen pregnancy by prohibiting

welfare to minor mothers and denying increased AFDC for additional children while on welfare, cut spending for welfare programs, and enact a tough two-years-and-out provision with work requirements to promote individual responsibility.

4. THE FAMILY REINFORCEMENT ACT: Child support enforcement, tax incentives for adoption, strengthening rights of parents in their children's education, stronger child pornography laws, and an elderly dependent care tax credit to reinforce the central role of families in American society.

5. THE AMERICAN DREAM RESTORATION ACT: A S500 per child tax credit, begin repeal of the marriage tax penalty, and creation of American Dream Savings Accounts to provide middle class tax relief.

6. THE NATIONAL SECURITY RESTORATION ACT: No U.S. troops under U.N. command and restoration of the essential parts of our national security funding to strengthen our national defense and maintain our credibility around the world.

7. THE SENIOR CITIZENS FAIRNESS ACT: Raise the Social Security earnings limit which currently forces seniors out of the work force, repeal the 1993 tax hikes on Social Security benefits and provide tax incentives for private long-term care insurance to let Older Americans keep more of what they have earned over the years.

8. THE JOB CREATION AND WAGE ENHANCEMENT ACT: Small business incentives, capital gains cut and indexation, neutral cost recovery, risk assessment/cost-benefit analysis, strengthening the Regulatory Flexibility Act and unfunded mandate reform to create jobs and raise worker wages.

9. THE COMMON SENSE LEGAL REFORM ACT:
"Loser pays" laws, reasonable limits on punitive damages
and reform of product liability laws to stem the endless tide
of litigation.

10. THE CITIZEN LEGISLATURE ACT: A first-ever
vote on term limits to replace career politicians with citizen
legislators.

Further, we will instruct the House Budget Committee to
report to the floor and we will work to enact additional
budget savings, beyond the budget cuts specifically included
in the legislation described above, to ensure that the Federal
budget deficit will be less than it would have been without
the enactment of these bills.

Respecting the judgment of our fellow citizens as we seek
their mandate for reform, we hereby pledge our names to
this Contract with America.

Source: U.S. House of Representatives

John Adams, Notes for an Oration at

Braintree,

Spring of 1722

The Origin, the Nature, the Principles and the Ends of
Government, in all Ages, the ignorant as well as the
enlightened, and in all Nations, the barbarous as well as
civilized, have employed the Wits of ingenious Men.
The Magi, the Mufti, the Bramins, and Brachmans,
Mandarines, Rabbies, Philosophers, Divines, Schoolmen,
Hermits, Legislators, Politicians, Lawyers, have made these
the subjects of their Enquiries and Reasonings.
There is nothing too absurd, nothing too enthusiastical (sic)
or superstitious, nothing too wild or whimsical, nothing too
prophane (sic) or impious, to be found among such
Thinkers, upon such Subjects. Any Thing which subtelty
(sic) could investigate or imagination conceive, would serve
for an Hypothesis, to support a System, excepting only what
alone can support the System of Truth—Nature, and
Experience.
The Science of Government, like all other Sciences, is best
pursued by Observation And Experiment—Remark the
Phenomina (sic) of Nature, and from these deduce the
Principles and Ends of Government.
Men are the Objects of this Science, as much as Air, Fire,
Earth and Water, are the Objects of Phylosophy (sic), Points,
Lines, Surfaces and Solids of Geometry, or the Sun, Moon
and Stars of Astronomy. Human Nature therefore and
human Life must be carefully observed and studied. Here we
should spread before Us a Map of Man—view him in
different Soils and Climates, in different Nations and

Countries, under different Religions and Customs, in Barbarity and Civility, in a {p. 57} State of Ignorance and enlightened with Knowledge, in Slavery and in freedom, in Infancy and Age.

He will be found, a rational, sensible and social Animal, in all. The Instinct of Nature impells him to Society, and Society causes the Necessity of Government.

Government is nothing more than the combined Force of Society, or the united Power of the Multitude, for the Peace, Order, Safety, Good and Happiness of the People, who compose the Society. There is no King or Queen Bee distinguished from all others, by Size or Figure, or beauty and Variety of Colours (sic), in the human Hive. No Man has yet produced any Revelation from Heaven in his favour (sic), any divine Communication to govern his fellow Men. Nature throws us all into the World equall (sic) and alike. Nor has any Form of Government the Honour of a divine original or Appointment. The Author of Nature has left it wholly in the Choice of the People, to make what mutual Covenants, to erect what Kind of Governments, and to exalt what Persons they please to power and dignities, for their own Ease, Convenience and Happiness.

Government being according to my Definition the collected Strength of all for the general Good of all, Legislators have devised a Great Variety of forms in which this Strength may be arranged.

There are only Three simple Forms of Government.

When the whole Power of the Society is lodged in the Hands of the whole Society, the Government is called a Democracy, or the Rule of the Many.

When the Sovereignty, or Supreme Power is placed in the Hands of a few great, rich, wise Men, the Government is an Aristocracy, or the Rule of the few. (Emphasis added)

When the absolute Power of the Community is entrusted to the Discretion of a single Person, the Government is called a Monarchy, or the Rule of one, in this Case the whole Legislative and Executive Power is in the Breast of one Man.

There are however two other Kinds of Monarchies. One is when the supreme Power is not in a single Person but in the Laws, the Administration being committed solely to the Prince.

Another Kind is a limited Monarchy, where the Nobles or the Commons or both have a Check upon all the Acts of Legislation of the Prince.

There is an indefinite Variety of other Forms of Government, occasioned by different Combinations of the Powers of Society, and {p. 58} different Intermixtures of these Forms of Government, one with another.

The best Governments of the World have been mixed.

The Republics of Greece, Rome, Carthage, were all mixed Governments. The English, Dutch and Swiss, enjoy the Advantages of mixed Governments at this Day.

Sometimes Kings have courted the People in Opposition to the Nobles. At other Times the Nobles have united with the People in Opposition to Kings. But Kings and Nobles have much oftener combined together, to crush, to humble and to Fleece the People.

But this is an unalterable Truth, that the People can never be enslaved but by their own Tameness, Pusillanimity, Sloth or Corruption.

They may be deceived, and their Symplicity (sic), Ignorance, and Docility render them frequently liable to deception. And of this, the aspiring, designing, ambitious few are very sensible. He is the Statesman qualifyed (sic) by Nature to scatter Ruin and Destruction in his Path who by deceiving a Nation can render Despotism desirable in their Eyes and make himself popular in Undoing.

The Preservation of Liberty depends upon the intellectual and moral Character of the People. As long as Knowledge and Virtue are diffused generally among the Body of a Nation, it is impossible they should be enslaved. This can be brought to pass only by debasing their Understandings, or by corrupting their Hearts.

What is the Tendency of the late Innovations? The Severity, the Cruelty of the late Revenue Laws, and the Terrors of the formidable Engine, contrived to execute them, the Court of

Admiralty? Is not the natural and necessary Tendency of these Innovations, to introduce dark Intrigues, Insincerity, Simulation, Bribery and Perjury, among Custom house officers, Merchants, Masters, Mariners and their Servants? What is the Tendency, what has been the Effect of introducing a standing Army into our Metropolis? Have we not seen horrid Rancour (sic), furious Violence, infernal Cruelty, shocking Impiety and Profanation, and shameless, abandoned Debauchery, running down the Streets like a Stream?

Liberty, under every conceivable Form of Government is always in Danger. It is so even under a simple, or perfect Democracy, more so {p. 59} under a mixed Government, like the Republic of Rome, and still more so under a limited Monarchy.

Ambition is one of the more ungovernable Passions of the human Heart. The Love of Power, is insatiable and uncontroulable (sic).

Even in the simple Democracies of ancient Greece, Jealous as they were of Power, even their Ostracism could not always preserve them from the grasping Desires and Designs, from the overbearing Popularity, of their great Men.

Even Rome, in her wisest and most virtuous Period, from the Expulsion of her Kings to the Overthrow of the Commonwealth, was always in Danger from the Power of some and the Turbulence, Faction and Popularity of others. There is Danger from all Men. The only Maxim of a free Government, ought to be to trust no Man living, with Power to endanger the public Liberty.

In England, the common Rout to Power has been by making clamorous Professions of Patriotism, in early Life, to secure a great Popularity, and to ride upon that Popularity, into the highest Offices of State, and after they have arrived there, they have been generally found, as little zealous to preserve the Constitution, as their Predecessors whom they have hunted down.

The Earl of Strafford, in early Life, was a mighty Patriot and Anti-courtier.

Sir Robert Walpole. Commited (sic) to the Tower the Father of Corruption.

Harley also, a great and bold Advocate for the Constitution and Liberties of his Country.

But I need not go to Greece or to Rome, or to Britain for Examples. There are Persons now living in this Province, who for a long Course of their younger Years, professed and were believed to be the Guardian Angells (sic) of our civil and Religious Liberties, whose latter Conduct, since they have climbed up by Popularity to Power, has exhibited as great a Contrast to their former Professions and Principles, as ever was seen in a Strafford, an Harley, or a Walpole.

Be upon your Guard then, my Countrymen.

We see, by the Sketches I have given you, that all the great Kingdoms of Europe have once been free. But that they have lost their Liberties, by the Ignorance, the Weakness, the Inconstancy, and Disunion of the People. Let Us guard against these dangers, let us be firm and stable, as wise as Serpents and as harmless as Doves, but as daring and intrepid as Heroes. Let Us cherish the Means of Knowl• {p. 60} edge—our schools and Colledges (sic)—let Us cherish our Militia, and encourage military Discipline and skill.

The English Nation have been more fortunate than France, Spain, or any other—for the Barons, the Grandees, the Nobles, instead of uniting with [the] Crown, to suppress the People, united with the People, and struggled vs. the Crown, untill (sic) they obtained the great Charter, which was but a Restoration and Confirmation of the Laws and Constitution of our Saxon King Edward the Confessor.

Liberty depends upon an exact Balance (sic), a nice Counterpoise of all the Powers of the state.3

When the Popular Power becomes grasping, and eager after Augmentation, or for Amplification, beyond its proper Weight, or Line, it becomes as dangerous as any other. Sweeden (sic) is an Example.

The Independency of the Governor, his Salary granted by the Crown, out of a Revenue extorted from this People.

The Refusal of the Governor to consent to any Act for granting a Salary to the Agent, unless chosen by the 3 Branches of the General Court.

The Instruction to the Governor, not to consent to any Tax Bill unless certain Crown Officers are exempted.

The Multiplication of Offices and Officers among Us.

The Revenue, arising from Duties upon Tea, Sugar, Molasses and other Articles, &c.

It is the popular Power, the democraticall (sic) Branch of our Constitution that is invaded.

If K[ing], Lords and Commons, can make Laws to bind Us in all Cases whatsoever, The People here will have no Influence, no Check, no Power, no Controul, no Negative. And the Government we are under, instead of being a mixture of Monarchy, Aristocracy and Democracy, will be a Mixture only of Monarchy and Aristocracy. For the Lords and Commons may be considered equally with Regard to Us as Nobles, as the few, as Aristocratical (sic) Grandees, independent of Us the People, uninfluenced by Us, having no fear of Us, nor Love for Us.

Wise and free Nations have made it their Rule, never to vote their Donations of Money to their Kings to enable them to carry on the Affairs of Government, untill they had Opportunities to examine the {p. 61} State of the Nation, and to remonstrate against Grievances and demand and obtain the Redress of them. This was the Maxim in France, Spain, Sweeden, Denmark, Poland, while those Nations were free. What Opportunities then shall we in this Province have to demand and obtain the Redress of Grievances, if our Governors and Judges and other Officers and Magistrates are to be supported by the Ministry, without the Gifts of the People.—Consider the Case of Barbadoes (sic) and Virginia. Their Governors have been made independent by the imprudent shortsighted Acts of their own Assemblies. What is the Consequence.

APPENDIX F

The "Tree of Liberty" letter

From Thomas Jefferson to William Smith

Paris, November 13, 1787

DEAR SIR, -- I am now to acknowledge (sic) the receipt of your favors of October the 4th, 8th, & 26th. In the last you apologise (sic) for your letters of introduction to Americans coming here. It is so far from needing apology on your part, that it calls for thanks on mine. I endeavor to show civilities to all the Americans who come here, & will give me opportunities of doing it: and it is a matter of comfort to know from a good quarter what they are, & how far I may go in my attentions to them. Can you send me Woodmason's bills for the two copying presses for the M. de la Fayette, & the M. de Chastellux? The latter makes one article in a considerable account, of old standing, and which I cannot present for want of this article. -- I do not know whether it is to yourself or Mr. Adams I am to give my thanks for the copy of the new constitution. I beg leave through you to place them where due. It will be yet three weeks before I shall receive them from America. There are very good articles in it: & very bad. I do not know which preponderate. What we have lately read in the history of Holland, in the chapter on the Stadtholder, would have sufficed to set me against a chief magistrate eligible for a long duration, if I had ever been disposed towards one: & what we have always read of the elections of Polish kings should have forever excluded the idea of one continuable (sic) for life. Wonderful is the effect of impudent & persevering lying. The British ministry have so long hired their gazetteers to repeat and model into every form lies about our being in anarchy, that the world has at length believed them, the English nation has believed them, the ministers themselves have come to believe them, & what is more wonderful, we have believed them ourselves. Yet where does this anarchy exist? Where did it ever exist, except in the single instance of Massachusetts? And can history produce an instance of rebellion so honourably (sic) conducted? I say nothing of it's motives. They were founded in ignorance, not wickedness. God forbid we should ever be 20 years without such a rebellion. The people cannot be all, & always well informed. The part which is wrong will be discontented in proportion to the importance of the facts they misconceive. If they remain quiet under such misconceptions it is a lethargy, the forerunner of death to the public liberty. We have had 13. states independent 11. years. There has been one rebellion. That comes to one rebellion in a century & a half for each state. What country before ever existed a century & a half without a rebellion? & what country can preserve it's liberties if their rulers are not warned from time to time that their people preserve the spirit of resistance? Let them take arms. The remedy is to set them right as to facts, pardon & pacify them. What signify a few lives lost in a century or two? The tree of liberty must be refreshed from time to time with the blood of patriots & tyrants. It is it's natural manure. Our Convention has been too much impressed by the insurrection of Massachusetts: and in the spur of the moment they are setting up a kite to keep the hen-yard in order. I hope in God this article will be rectified before the new constitution is accepted. -- You ask me if any thing (sic) transpires here on the subject of S. America? Not a word. I know that there are combustible materials there, and that they wait the torch only. But this country probably will join the extinguishers. -- The want of facts worth communicating to you has occasioned me to give a little loose to dissertation. We must be contented to amuse, when we cannot inform.

The Federalist No. 39

Conformity of the Plan to Republican Principles

Independent Journal
Wednesday, January 16, 1788
[James Madison]

To the People of the State of New York:

THE last paper having concluded the observations which were meant to introduce a candid survey of the plan of government reported by the convention, we now proceed to the execution of that part of our undertaking.

The first question that offers itself is, whether the general form and aspect of the government be strictly republican. It is evident that no other form would be reconcilable with the genius of the people of America; with the fundamental principles of the Revolution; or with that honorable determination which animates every votary of freedom, to rest all our political experiments on the capacity of mankind for self-government. If the plan of the convention, therefore, be found to depart from the republican character, its advocates must abandon it as no longer defensible.

What, then, are the distinctive characters of the republican form? Were an answer to this question to be sought, not by recurring to principles, but in the application of the term by political writers, to the constitution of different States, no satisfactory one would ever be found. Holland, in which no particle of the supreme authority is derived from the people, has passed almost universally under the denomination of a republic. The same title has been bestowed on Venice, where absolute power over the great body of the people is exercised, in the most absolute manner, by a small body of hereditary nobles. Poland, which is a mixture of aristocracy and of monarchy in their worst forms, has been dignified with the same appellation. The government of England, which has one republican branch only, combined with an hereditary aristocracy and monarchy, has, with equal impropriety, been frequently placed on the list of republics. These examples, which are nearly as dissimilar to each other as to a genuine republic, show the extreme inaccuracy with which the term has been used in political disquisitions.

If we resort for a criterion to the different principles on which different forms of government are established, we may define a republic to be, or at least may bestow that name on, a government which derives all its powers directly or indirectly from the great body of the people, and is administered by persons holding their offices during pleasure, for a limited period, or during good behavior. It is *essential* to such a government that it be derived from the great body of the society, not from an inconsiderable proportion, or a favored class of it; otherwise a handful of tyrannical nobles, exercising their oppressions by a delegation of their powers, might aspire to the rank of republicans, and claim for their government the honorable title of republic. It is *sufficient* for such a government that the persons administering it be appointed, either directly or indirectly, by the people; and that they hold their appointments by either of the tenures just specified; otherwise every government in the United States, as well as every other popular government that has been or can be well organized or well executed, would be degraded from the republican character. According to the constitution of every State in the Union, some or other of the officers of government are appointed indirectly only by the people. According to most of them, the chief magistrate himself is so appointed. And according to one, this mode of appointment is extended to one of the co-ordinate branches of the legislature. According to all the constitutions, also, the tenure of the highest offices is extended to a definite period, and in many instances, both within the legislative and executive departments, to a period of years. According to the provisions of most of the constitutions, again, as well as according to the most respectable and received opinions on the subject, the members of the judiciary department are to retain their offices by the firm tenure of good behavior.

On comparing the Constitution planned by the convention with the standard here fixed, we perceive at once that it is, in the most rigid sense, conformable to it. The House of Representatives, like that of one branch at least of all the State legislatures, is elected immediately by the great body of the people. The Senate, like the present Congress, and the Senate of Maryland, derives its appointment indirectly from the people. The President is indirectly derived from the choice of the people, according to the example in most of the States. Even the judges, with all other officers of the Union, will, as in the several States, be the choice, though a remote choice, of the people themselves, the duration of the appointments is equally conformable to the republican standard, and to the model of State constitutions The House of Representatives is periodically elective, as in all the States; and for the period of two years, as in the State of South Carolina. The Senate is elective, for the period of six years; which is but one year more than the period of the Senate of Maryland, and but two more than that of the Senates of New York and Virginia. The President is to continue in office for the period of four years; as in New York and Delaware, the chief magistrate is elected for three years, and in South Carolina for two years. In the other States the election is annual. In several of the States, however, no constitutional provision is made for the impeachment of the chief magistrate. And in Delaware and

Virginia he is not impeachable till out of office. The President of the United States is impeachable at any time during his continuance in office. The tenure by which the judges are to hold their places, is, as it unquestionably ought to be, that of good behavior. The tenure of the ministerial offices generally, will be a subject of legal regulation, conformably to the reason of the case and the example of the State constitutions.

Could any further proof be required of the republican complexion of this system, the most decisive one might be found in its absolute prohibition of titles of nobility, both under the federal and the State governments; and in its express guaranty of the republican form to each of the latter.

"But it was not sufficient," say the adversaries of the proposed Constitution, "for the convention to adhere to the republican form. They ought, with equal care, to have preserved the *federal* form, which regards the Union as a *Confederacy* of sovereign states; instead of which, they have framed a *national* government, which regards the Union as a *consolidation* of the States." And it is asked by what authority this bold and radical innovation was undertaken? The handle which has been made of this objection requires that it should be examined with some precision.

Without inquiring into the accuracy of the distinction on which the objection is founded, it will be necessary to a just estimate of its force, first, to ascertain the real character of the government in question; secondly, to inquire how far the convention were authorized to propose such a government; and thirdly, how far the duty they owed to their country could supply any defect of regular authority.

First. In order to ascertain the real character of the government, it may be considered in relation to the foundation on which it is to be established; to the sources from which its ordinary powers are to be drawn; to the operation of those powers; to the extent of them; and to the authority by which future changes in the government are to be introduced.

On examining the first relation, it appears, on one hand, that the Constitution is to be founded on the assent and ratification of the people of America, given by deputies elected for the special purpose; but, on the other, that this assent and ratification is to be given by the people, not as individuals composing one entire nation, but as composing the distinct and independent States to which they respectively belong. It is to be the assent and ratification of the several States, derived from the supreme authority in each State, the authority of the people themselves. The act, therefore, establishing the Constitution, will not be a *national*, but a *federal* act.

That it will be a federal and not a national act, as these terms are understood by the objectors; the act of the people, as forming so many independent States, not as forming one aggregate nation, is obvious from this single consideration, that it is to result neither from the decision of a *majority* of the people of the Union, nor from that of a *majority* of the States. It must result from the *unanimous* assent of the several States that are parties to it, differing no otherwise from their ordinary assent than in its being expressed, not by the legislative authority, but by that of the people themselves. Were the people regarded in this transaction as forming one nation, the will of the majority of the whole people of the United States would bind the minority, in the same manner as the majority in each State must bind the minority; and the will of the majority must be determined either by a comparison of the individual votes, or by considering the will of the majority of the States as evidence of the will of a majority of the people of the United States. Neither of these rules have been adopted. Each State, in ratifying the Constitution, is considered as a sovereign body, independent of all others, and only to be bound by its own voluntary act. In this relation, then, the new Constitution will, if established, be a *federal*, and not a *national* constitution.

The next relation is, to the sources from which the ordinary powers of government are to be derived. The House of Representatives will derive its powers from the people of America; and the people will be represented in the same proportion, and on the same principle, as they are in the legislature of a particular State. So far the government is *national*, not *federal*. The Senate, on the other hand, will derive its powers from the States, as political and coequal societies; and these will be represented on the principle of equality in the Senate, as they now are in the existing Congress. So far the government is *federal*, not *national*. The executive power will be derived from a very compound source. The immediate election of the President is to be made by the States in their political characters. The votes allotted to them are in a compound ratio, which considers them partly as distinct and coequal societies, partly as unequal members of the same society. The eventual election, again, is to be made by that branch of the legislature which consists of the national representatives; but in this particular act they are to be thrown into the form of individual delegations, from so many distinct and coequal bodies politic. From this aspect of the government it appears to be of a mixed character, presenting at least as many *federal* as *national* features.

The difference between a federal and national government, as it relates to the *operation of the government*, is supposed to consist in this, that in the former the powers operate on the political bodies composing the Confederacy, in their political capacities; in the latter, on the individual citizens composing the nation, in their individual capacities. On trying the Constitution by this criterion, it falls under the *national*, not the *federal* character; though perhaps not so completely as has been understood. In several cases, and particularly in the trial of controversies to which States may be parties, they must be viewed and proceeded against in their collective and political capacities only. So far the national countenance of the government on this side seems to be disfigured by a few federal features. But this blemish is perhaps unavoidable in any plan; and the operation of the government on the people, in their individual capacities, in its ordinary and most essential proceedings, may, on the whole, designate it, in this relation, a *national* government.

But if the government be national with regard to the *operation* of its powers, it changes its aspect again when we contemplate it in relation to the *extent* of its powers. The idea of a national government involves in it, not only an authority over the individual citizens, but an indefinite supremacy over all persons and things, so far as they are objects of lawful government. Among a people consolidated into one nation, this supremacy is completely vested in the national legislature. Among communities united for particular purposes, it is vested partly in the general and partly in the municipal legislatures. In the former case, all local authorities are subordinate to the supreme; and may be controlled, directed, or abolished by it at pleasure. In the latter, the local or municipal authorities form distinct and independent portions of the supremacy, no more subject, within their respective spheres, to the general authority, than the general authority is subject to them, within its own sphere. In this relation, then, the proposed government cannot be deemed a *national* one; since its jurisdiction extends to certain enumerated objects only, and leaves to the several States a residuary and inviolable sovereignty over all other objects. It is true that in controversies relating to the boundary between the two jurisdictions, the tribunal which is ultimately to decide, is to be established under the general government. But this does not change the principle of the case. The decision is to be impartially made, according to the rules of the Constitution; and all the usual and most effectual precautions are taken to secure this impartiality. Some such tribunal is clearly essential to prevent an appeal to the sword and a dissolution of the compact; and that it ought to be established under the general rather than under the local governments, or, to speak more properly, that it could be safely established under the first alone, is a position not likely to be combated.

If we try the Constitution by its last relation to the authority by which amendments are to be made, we find it neither wholly *national* nor wholly *federal*. Were it wholly national, the supreme and ultimate authority would reside in the *majority* of the people of the Union; and this authority would be competent at all times, like that of a majority of every national society, to alter or abolish its established government. Were it wholly federal, on the other hand, the concurrence of each State in the Union would be essential to every alteration that would be binding on all. The mode provided by the plan of the convention is not founded on either of these principles. In requiring more than a majority, and particularly in computing the proportion by *States*, not by *citizens*, it departs from the *national* and advances towards the *federal* character; in rendering the concurrence of less than the whole number of States sufficient, it loses again the *federal* and partakes of the *national* character.

The proposed Constitution, therefore, [even when tested by the rules laid down by its antagonists,] is, in strictness, neither a national nor a federal Constitution, but a composition of both. In its foundation it is federal, not national; in the sources from which the ordinary powers of the government are drawn, it is partly federal and partly national; in the operation of these powers, it is national, not federal; in the extent of them, again, it is federal, not national; and, finally, in the

authoritative mode of introducing amendments, it is neither wholly federal nor wholly national.

Publius